Buddhism

WORLD RELIGIONS

Buddhism

SERINITY YOUNG

Marshall Cavendish
Benchmark
New York

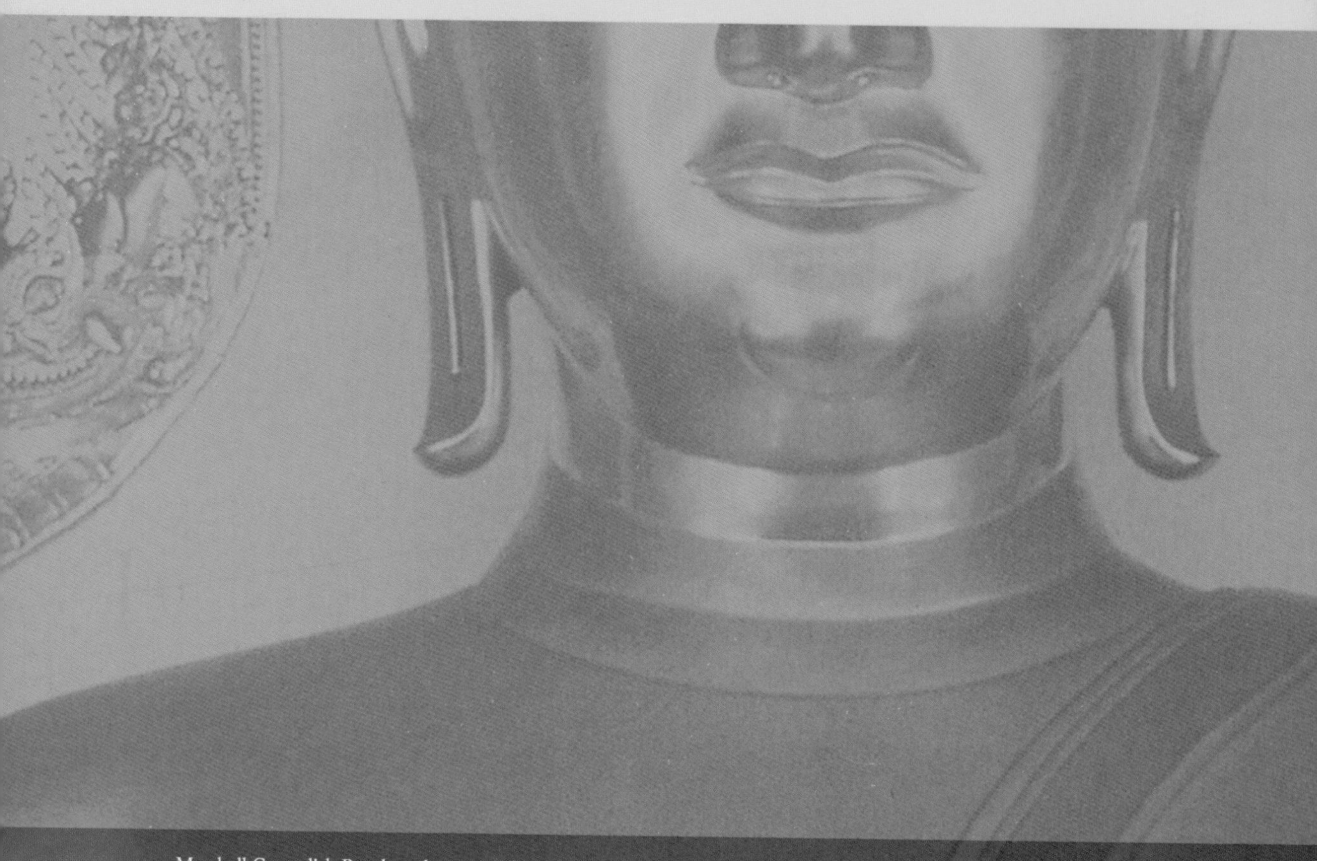

Marshall Cavendish Benchmark • 99 White Plains Road • Tarrytown, NY 10591-9001 • www.marshallcavendish.us

• Library of Congress Cataloging-in-Publication Data • Young, Serinity. • Buddhism / by Serinity Young. • p. cm. — (World religions) • Includes bibliographical references and index. • Summary: "Provides an overview of the history and origins, basic tenets and beliefs, organizations, traditions, customs, rites, societal and historical influences, and modern-day impact of Buddhism"—Provided by publisher. • ISBN-13: 978-0-7614-2114-6 • ISBN-10: 0-7614-2114-9 • 1. Buddhism. I. Title. II. Series. • BQ4012.Y68 2006 • 294.3—dc22 • 2005016880 • Series design by Sonia Chaghatzbanian
Photo research by Candlepants, Incorporated

Cover photo: Ladislav Janicek/zefa/Corbis • The photographs in this book are used by permission and through the courtesy of: *Corbis*: Ladislav Janicek/zefa: 1, 3, 4, 6–7, 10, 14, 24, 27, 31, 40, 43, 64, 77; Archivo Iconographico, S.A., 11; B.S.P.I., 13; Richard Bickel, 16; Luca I. Tettoni, 17; David Cumming, Eye Ubiquitous, 22; Macduff Everton, 26; Geray Sweeney, 42; David Samual Robbins, 49; H.Sitton/zefa, 52; Alison Wright, 92; Chris Lisle, 96; Emely/zefa, 98; C. Pierre Perrin/SYGMA, 101; Rob Howard, 103. *Getty Images*: Gavin Hellier, 2; John & Lisa Merrill, 8, back cover; Tony Latham, 20; Jeff Spielman, 65; Angelo Cavalli, 79. *Art Resource, NY*: Werner Forman, 32; Reunion des Musees Nationaux, 36; Alinari, 95. *SuperStock:* age fotostock, 38–39, 80–81.

Printed in China • 1 3 5 6 4 2

contents

Buddhism

A close-up of the all-seeing, compassionate eye of Buddha. This sculptural image comes from Ladakh in northern India.

one

THE LIFE OF THE BUDDHA

Early Life

Buddhism begins with the life of Gautama of the Shakya clan, later called the Buddha (a title meaning "the enlightened one"), who lived from about 566 to 486 B.C.E. His life has been recorded in texts, in works of art, and in pilgrimage sites throughout Asia. As a young man the Buddha is said to have led a carefree, luxurious life in which he was carefully protected from the harsher realities of human existence. His father, King Shuddhodana, conspired in this deception due to a dream the Buddha's mother, Queen Maya, had at the time of his conception. She dreamed a white elephant approached her, struck her right side with its trunk, and then entered her womb. When sages were consulted about the dream, they interpreted it to mean that Queen Maya was pregnant with a son who would become a *cakravartin*, either a great king or a great ascetic. *Cakra* means "wheel" and *vartin* means "someone who turns," so *cakravartin* means "a wheel turner." It refers to a chariot wheel, which is a symbol of military conquest—the activity of a king—and to spiritual conquest, which is the activity of an ascetic. The king conquers and embraces the world through physical strength; the ascetic conquers and rejects the world through spiritual strength.

Ascetics live apart from people, deep in the forests or on high mountains. They restrict their diets, avoid physical comforts, reject sexuality, and spend hours in deep meditation. When the Buddha's father heard the interpretation of Queen Maya's dream he became determined that his son would become a king, not an ascetic, so the king made life's pleasures the focus of Gautama's life. The king set about doing this by removing all unpleasant sights from the palace compound, including any elderly or sick people. Inevitably, Shuddhodana's plan broke down. When the Buddha was thirty years old, he was radically changed by four visions created by the gods. On four consecutive days he mounted his chariot and left through one of the four palace gates. Each day, during his ride, he experienced a different vision. On the first day, he saw an old man for the first time. On the second day, he saw a sick man, and on the third day, a dead man. These three visions introduced him to the reality of human suffering and to the transitory nature of human life. He had not known that human beings suffered and changed, that they became ill, grew old, and died. Even worse, the prevailing belief of his time was that people were reincarnated: on dying, they were reborn as other creatures who would suffer, grow old, and die again and again. From the Buddha's point of view, the suffering that accompanies being sick, growing old, and fearing death never ends. It is a cycle that repeats

The Wheel of Becoming

The wheel of becoming or rebirth is a frequent subject of Buddhist art. It shows what are called the six realms or destinies: the higher realms of the gods, humans, and demigods, and the lower realms of the hungry ghosts, hell beings, and animals held in the grasp of Mara, a demonic god who rules over beings motivated by desire. All living beings migrate through these six realms according to their good and bad karma, or deeds. Bad deeds lead to rebirth in a lower realm, good deeds to a higher realm. For instance, particularly good human beings can be reborn among the gods. The gods, however, are also trapped on this wheel—eventually they too die and are reborn in lower existences as human beings or even animals, because the good karma that earned them such a high rebirth wears out. This is good news for those in lower realms because eventually their bad karma will run out and they will be reborn in a higher realm. It explains as well why the gods help the Buddha; they want to get off the wheel, too.

Queen Maya is featured in this eighteenth-century sculpture.

again and again. His fourth vision, that of a male ascetic, presented him with a solution to the problem of suffering and impermanence raised by the first three visions. He decided to leave home, become an ascetic, and seek a way to liberate himself from the cycle of birth, death, and rebirth.

The story of the Buddha's four visions is filled with meaning for Buddhists. It expresses the Buddha's shock on discovering human suffering and is meant to awaken those who hear the story to the realization that they, too, like the Buddha, live as if such suffering does not exist. Biographies of the Buddha stress that he was a handsome and pampered prince, a young man of overly refined sensitivities. This makes his shock real, so that we can comprehend how these four encounters changed his life. The story tries to make us understand that if we, too, truly looked reality in the face, as the Buddha did through these visions, we would recoil from the pleasures of life. We would ask, as he did, is this all there is, or is there something beyond what we now know, a way out of the inevitable suffering of growing old, being ill, and dying? In this way, as the Buddha begins his spiritual search, the story invites us to join him.

The story lingers over what the Buddha gave up, particularly his involvement with women. One of his earliest biographies, the *Lalitavistara*, from now on referred to as the *LV*, was composed anonymously around the beginning of the Common Era, although it contains much earlier tales that were passed down orally. It refers to this period of the Buddha's life as when he "resided in the women's quarters," sometimes translated as "the harem." When the Buddha prepared to leave home and abandon a life of comfort and ease, he abandoned the beauty and charms of the harem women and he completely rejected women.

When the Buddha left home he also left civilization, seeking the solitude of the untamed forests of India. The first thing he did was to

The head of a young novice is shaved before his Buddhist ordination ceremony.

cut off his long hair. He then discarded his royal robes for the rough cloth of an ascetic and picked up a small bowl with which he would beg for his food. Today, when monks are ordained they imitate these actions of the Buddha: they shave their heads, put on ascetic robes, and go begging for their food.

The Buddha lived in a time of religious turmoil when many people were seeking spiritual truths in forests and on mountains. Among these seekers he found several spiritual teachers, and he began to practice severe austerities that he believed would free the spirit from the body. He tried exposing his body to the sun and wind and barely

Merit

Merit is an important Buddhist concept. People receive merit by offering food and clothing to nuns and monks or by chanting, going on pilgrimages, and the like. The merit they gain enriches their own spiritual futures and may bring them good rebirths. Merit can also be dedicated to someone else, as when people dedicate their merit to the welfare of all the beings in the world. Most often, people dedicate their merit to the spiritual welfare of their deceased parents in the hope that their parents will receive good rebirths. Many Asians believe that children are indebted to their parents for having given them life and for caring for them while they were infants, and this sense of indebtedness extends into the afterlife.

eating enough food to stay alive. By some accounts, he ate only one grain of rice, one juniper berry, and one sesame seed a day during this period. The Buddha's determination in following this path attracted five male disciples, but after six years of such austerities he looked like a corpse, and the gods who were watching over him feared he would die. Filled with concern, they turned to his mother, Queen Maya, who had died seven days after the Buddha's birth and lived among the gods. Once she learned about her son's condition, Maya appeared before the Buddha and reminded him of his miraculous conception and the prediction of his future spiritual greatness. She cautioned him that all this was at risk because of his continued austerities. The Buddha reassured her that he would attain his goal, and she returned to heaven. Buddha changed his spiritual practices, returning to the world and to women.

Realizing that his body was too weak to achieve enlightenment, he decided to eat solid food. His five male disciples took this to mean that he had abandoned asceticism, and they deserted him. But some young village women came by and one of them, Sujata, offered him a dish of rice and milk, which he accepted. In accepting this food, the Buddha also began to accept women. He began reversing his earlier rejection of them. The contrast between the behavior of his male disciples, who deserted him, and the village women, who nurtured him, is remarkable.

After eating the food, the Buddha looked for something to replace the tattered robe he had worn for six years. Entering a cemetery, he picked up a cloth that had been used to wrap the body of a dead woman. Next he wanted to bathe, so the gods created a pond for him. When he finished his bath and tried to step out of the pond, though, the powerful and demonic god Mara caused the water to rise. The Buddha then asked the goddess of a nearby tree to bend down a branch so he could pull himself out, which she did.

The next day Sujata invited the Buddha to a meal in her home. Here he re-entered the women's quarters, re-entered the world of everyday people, and once again accepted food offerings from a woman. His biography describes this as a fortunate event. The Buddha thought: "'Now that Sujata has offered such food to me, there can be no doubt: after partaking of it, I will attain the perfect, supreme, and complete Enlightenment of a Buddha.'" He called her "my sister" and gave her spiritual teachings. After leaving Sujata's house, he bathed in a river where a female *naga* (a semi-divine snakelike creature) offered him a throne as a sign that he would soon become enlightened. Restored by once more accepting all aspects of the feminine, the Buddha took a seat under the Bo Tree, the place where he would achieve enlightenment.

The *LV* presents an intriguing sequence of female characters: a woman who is dead yet lives (Maya), living women (the village women), a dead woman (the corpse), and semi-divine women (the tree goddess and the female *naga*). All these females, in their various states of existence, whether living or dead, human or divine, are able to aid the Buddha in some way. In his first lengthy contact with women since his initial rejection of them, the Buddha established a role in Buddhism for women who were not nuns, that of being donors. The appointment of this role developed into the belief that laypeople who are unable to become monks or nuns can still acquire merit that will enable them to attain enlightenment in a future lifetime.

The earth-touching pose represents the earth siding with the Buddha against Mara and his legions of demons. It is the main iconographic representation of the Buddha's supreme achievement, enlightenment, and this gesture, or mudra, comes to represent that state.

As the Buddha sat under the Bo Tree, Mara—the demonic god of the realm of desire—challenged the Buddha's passage beyond Mara's realm to an enlightened state. He sent an army of demons to torment and frighten the Buddha, but they did not succeed. Mara directly confronted the Buddha by asking: "Through what merit will you gain deliverance?" The Buddha answered:

I have freely made hundreds of millions of offerings. I have cut off my hands, my feet, my eyes, and my head as gifts for those who wished them; ardently desiring the deliverance of beings, I distributed houses, riches, seeds, beds, garments, gardens, and parks to all who asked.

Still, Mara was not satisfied by the Buddha's answer, and the god demanded a witness. The Buddha then called upon the earth to be his witness by touching it with his right hand. The earth responded first by trembling, and then the goddess of the earth is said to have "revealed the upper half of her body" and have spoken as a witness for the Buddha.

The earth-touching pose represents the earth siding with the Buddha against Mara and his many demons and is one of the most popular images of the historical Buddha (See the cover of this

The Bo Tree

Bo is short for *Bodhi*, meaning "enlightenment," so the Bo Tree is the tree of enlightenment. It is a papal tree, a long-lived species of fig tree. Some bo trees live for more than a thousand years, and faithful Buddhists believe that the actual tree under which the Buddha achieved enlightenment still exists. This tree grows at Bodh Gaya, the most important Buddhist pilgrimage site and the center of the Buddhist world. It is the focus of intense devotion.

The most frequent form of devotion at Bodh Gaya is to circumambulate (walk in a circle around) the Bo Tree, with one's right side toward it, while offering prayers. Other devotees light candles and make offerings of flowers or burning sticks of incense. Some people do full-body prostrations: they lie flat on the ground, stretching their arms forward with their palms joined together in devotion, and mark the spot where their hands touch the ground. They then rise, walk the few steps to that spot, and once again lie down. Having a goal of ten thousand prostrations is not uncommon. Today Buddhists from all over the world visit Bodh Gaya.

book). It is the main artistic representation of the Buddha's supreme achievement: enlightenment. The gesture of his right hand extending downward to touch the earth signals the necessary female part of that achievement. This gesture, or mudra, came to represent the state of enlightenment.

Buddha's Enlightenment

After Mara was defeated by the Buddha's accumulated merit and steadfast purpose, the Buddha remained under the Bo Tree and entered a deep state of meditation that lasted all night. In the first part of the night, he developed the ability to see many beings in the process of being born, dying, and passing into new births according to their good and bad karma. In the middle of the night, he was able to remember all his previous lives:

> **I was such and such a person, my name was this, my race was this, my lineage this; my color was this, the food I ate was such and such, this the span of life, this the length of time that I remained there; this was the happiness and unhappiness which I experienced. And then after leaving that life, I was born such and such a person; having passed on, I was born such and such a person; having passed on, I was born here. He remembered exactly the places and circumstances of his own lives and those of all other beings.**

In the last part of the night, just before dawn, the Buddha reflected on the suffering endured by people being born, growing old, and dying again and again. He asked himself how this cycle could be broken; how suffering could end. He came to realize that desire caused suffering, the desire that things be different than they are. For instance, the desire not to die creates suffering because that is everyone's fate.

The Buddha also became aware that if one could stop desiring, then suffering would cease. Indeed the desire to be reborn would cease, and one would be free of the wheel of rebirth. Meditating on this new understanding, just as dawn broke, the Buddha achieved complete enlightenment.

what the Buddha Taught

The Buddha spent several days sitting under the Bo Tree in his new state of awareness. But then he realized that he could not teach what he had learned because it was too difficult to grasp. The great gods Brahma and Indra then went to Buddha and pleaded with him to teach others what he had realized. The Buddha gave in because he knew that some people could learn from him. The first people he decided to teach were his former five male disciples. He thought he could teach them he saw that "they [were] endowed with good conduct and [had] gathered pure teachings; they [were] turned toward the path of deliverance and [were] free from all hindrances." In other words, they led moral lives and were committed to achieving enlightenment. With the divine vision he had gained from achieving enlightenment, he saw that the five men were gathered together in the Deer Park in the village of Sarnath, a short distance from the holy Indian city of Benares (today called Varanasi). He went there, wearing a monk's robes, with shaved head, and carrying a begging bowl.

The Deer Park was an animal preserve, a place where deer were safe from hunters. Because it was so beautiful and peaceful, it also attracted ascetics who were searching for enlightenment.

At first the five former disciples were reluctant to show the Buddha any respect or courtesy, but his power and beauty were so great that they arose, greeted him properly, and welcomed him. In an instant their clothing was changed into that of Buddhist monks, their heads were shaved, and they held begging bowls. This is the first ordination

As part of the ordination of Buddhist monks, their heads are shaved and they are given a begging bowl to hold the food they are expected to procure.

ceremony of Buddhist monks, and it also demonstrates how the enlightenment experience transformed the Buddha from a mere mortal into a being with supernatural knowledge, abilities, and beauty.

That night the Buddha and his five disciples meditated together, and then the Buddha spoke to them. First, he told them to avoid the extremes of asceticism as well as the comforts of a worldly life. Instead he recommended a middle path between the two: avoiding the world and its comforts and problems but accepting offerings of food and clothing from laypeople. The Buddha's point was that enlightenment requires a healthy body, not a starved or an overfed one. It also requires a mind free of worldly cares, so the Buddha told his disciples not to have families and to remain celibate.

He then taught them the Four Noble Truths:
First, to live is to suffer.
Second, the cause of suffering is desire.
Third, when desire stops, suffering ceases.
Fourth, the way to stop desiring is to follow the Eightfold Path.

The Eightfold Path is part of the middle path and is designed to weaken the power of desire by moderate conscious living. The Eightfold Path involves right view, right intention, right speech, right action, right livelihood, right effort, right mindfulness, and right concentration. To follow the Eightfold Path requires knowing what is right and having the intention to do right in speech, in action, and in earning a living. For instance, a Buddhist would not work as a butcher because he or she does not believe in harming other beings. Right effort, right mindfulness, and right concentration refer to mental states: these require effort, being attentive at all times, and building a strong meditation practice. One makes the effort to be attentive while walking, sitting, eating, dressing, washing, and doing everything else.

Generally, the first step in meditation practice is to quiet the mind. Many Buddhists do this by sitting with a straight back and completely focusing their attention on their breaths. They notice if the breaths are deep or shallow, long or short, and they begin to gently slow down their breathing until it is deep and rhythmic. If, during the meditation, their mind drifts to a desired object, a problem, or something else, they gently refocus it on their breathing. They then sit completely still with a newly quieted mind, sometimes for hours.

After listening to the Buddha's first sermon, the five disciples achieved enlightenment, and the *LV* ends. Other early biographies of the Buddha tell of his long life—the Buddha lived to be eighty

The Mahabodhi Temple

The Mahabodhi Temple was built close to the Bo Tree. In the nineteenth century a British archaeologist reconstructed it to its approximate form in the fifth century, though an even earlier structure marked this site. It has been a Buddhist site of pilgrimage from at least the third century B.C.E., if not before.

years old—during which he performed miracles, converted many laypeople, and created the monastic orders of nuns and monks. The first nuns were women from the Buddha's own family. The monastics and the laity are connected by the merit gained by the laypeople by giving donations: in this way the monastics receive food and clothing while the laity receives merit that will lead to their enlightenment in a future life. The Buddha required the nuns and monks to do without fixed homes. Instead they were encouraged to wander far and wide, spreading Buddhism. So, from its earliest days, Buddhism was a missionary religion. It sought converts in ever-widening circles throughout Asia, and in the nineteenth century it began to take root in Western countries as well.

The first step in becoming a Buddhist, whether as a monastic or a layperson, is to take refuge in the Three Jewels. The Three Jewels are the Buddha, the Dharma (his teachings), and the *Sangha* (the community of Buddhist monastics and the laity). Taking refuge marks an individual's understanding that the path to salvation lies with the Buddha, his teachings, and within the interactive community of monastics and its lay supporters. Laypeople also adopt five precepts: not to take any life (animal or human), not to steal, not to have illicit sex, not to lie, and not to use intoxicating substances. Monastics also adopt these five precepts, except that they more specifically take the vow of celibacy. Additionally, they do not eat after noon, which requires them to do their round of begging for food early in the morning. Nor do they adorn themselves, and they sit and sleep on mats on the ground rather than on high chairs or beds.

Most of this description of the early Buddhist community remains in place today except that monasteries became established communities, which limited the practice of wandering monks and nuns, and the goal of enlightenment was eventually seen as less attainable in one lifetime. So some monastics and most lay practitioners began to

Visakha, the Buddha's birthday

According to his biographies, the Buddha was born, achieved enlightenment, and died on the same date in different years. The months of the Asian calendar are connected to the cycle of the moon and therefore are different from Western months. For example, the month of Visakha corresponds to April or May. The Buddha's birthday, enlightenment, and death are celebrated on the full-moon day of Visakha. In Thailand it is celebrated in the evening, when people holding lighted candles and burning incense gather in monasteries to circumambulate the sacred shrines and place flowers before the Buddha's altar. They then listen to Buddha's life story, which may last all night.

concentrate on achieving a better future life. But for Buddhists, salvation still is achieved through the highly individual and personal experience of enlightenment. All people are believed capable of achieving enlightenment, but Buddhists generally believe that monks and nuns are in a better position to do so because they are free of the entanglements of worldly lives. One consequence of this emphasis on individual experience has been the value placed on the biographical literature of those individuals who achieved enlightenment and who provide an example for others.

Some of the earliest records of enlightenment are contained in the collected songs of the first generation of nuns and monks. These songs express spontaneous awakenings or breakthroughs in understanding, as were experienced by the five disciples after listening to the Buddha. The following poem attributed to the nun Patacara demonstrates that the experience comes to a mind disciplined by attentiveness and concentration.

One day, bathing my feet, I sit and watch
The water as it trickles down the slope.
Then I steadied my mind as one does a noble horse.
Going to my cell, I take my lamp,
And seated on my bed I watch the flame.
With a pin I pull the wick down into the oil.
The lamp goes out: Enlightenment.
My mind is freed.

The Death of the Buddha

Another major Buddhist pilgrimage site is Kushinigara, the place of the Buddha's death or the place of his entrance into nirvana. Buddhists call the world we know, the world of existence, *samsara*. This is within the realm of the wheel of rebirth. Its opposite, nirvana, is non-existence, the end of rebirth. When the Buddha ceased to breathe, he entered a state of non-being. He was extinguished, freed from the cycle of existence. He was beyond the many heavens and hells associated with the afterlife. Despite this, while he lay dying, the Buddha is believed to have said: "There are four places which the believing person should visit with feelings of reverence and awe. The places of [my] birth, . . . enlightenment, first sermon, . . . and death." So he established the four major Buddhist pilgrimage sites. He also said that his bodily remains were to be put in the hands of the laity who should burn his body on a funeral pyre. Whatever remained afterward, the relics of his body, was to be placed inside a stupa. According to traditional accounts, the relics of the Buddha were divided and distributed among stupas throughout the Buddhist world.

Stupas are cylindrical or rounded solid structures that house the bodily relics of the Buddha or of other important Buddhist figures. They are found throughout the Buddhist world, especially at pilgrimage sites and are the focus of worship. The relics of the Buddha were believed to be his actual living presence, thus stupas are worshipped in the same way that a living Buddha would be honored or worshipped. Devotions to both the person and the person's relics are believed to grant merit to the one who is praying. Buddhists visit stupas to ritually circumambulate them, offer incense and flowers, burn candles, and chant.

The sides of the first stone-and-brick stupas were decorated with carvings, as were the walkway railings that often surrounded them. The carvings depicted auspicious motifs and garlands and lotuses, such as tree gods, serpent beings, and guardian deities; along with illustrations

The huge Bodhanath Stupa, near Kathmandu, Nepal.

of the life of the Buddha and Buddhist saints, including episodes from the Buddha's past lives, the *jatakas*. The Buddha's life story was used to carve out a distinctly Buddhist sacred geography, one that devotees could contemplate when they journeyed to pilgrimage sites and circumambulated the stupas. Statues were also found at these sites, for example, life-sized images of the Buddha during his enlightenment and first sermon as well as Indian tree and river goddesses.

The images indicate that Buddhist pilgrimage sites were celebrations of both the esoteric experience of celibate enlightenment as well as the exoteric experience of happiness in this life, be it a good crop, a successful caravan, protection from misfortune, or a cure for childlessness. Individuals who visited these sites had a variety of goals, and some visitors were simply non-Buddhist tourists.

Commissioning religious artworks was another source of merit. Inscriptions added by donors to the images state that both monastics and the laity dedicated the merit obtained from such pious acts to the salvation of their deceased parents.

Another major site of Buddhist pilgrimage is the birthplace of the Buddha, the village of Lumbini in present-day Nepal. This site focuses on the Buddha's mother, Queen Maya, as well as on the Buddha himself.

Religion in the Time of the Buddha

People in India believed that earth and tree goddesses were generous deities who could grant fertility to people, cattle, and crops. The dieties were a source of wealth and power, and they answered the needs of ordinary people who tilled the soil, maintained herds, and hoped for children. They were easily absorbed into Buddhism, and the earliest known Buddhist pilgrimage sites (beginning in the third century B.C.E.) contained many images of these nature deities.

These goddesses were part of what came to be called Hinduism, but in the historical period of the Buddha is more accurately known as Brahmanism. This refers to the religion of the brahmans, the priests who performed sacrifices to the gods—most of whom were believed to live in various heavens, such as the one the Buddha's mother went to after she died.

two

DEVELOPMETNTS OF DOCTRINE

Asoka

An important element in the historical development of Buddhism was the reign of Emperor Asoka (third century B.C.E.), who became the model for all Buddhist kings. He is said to have converted to Buddhism after his bloody conquest of Kalinga (262 B.C.E.), which solidified his rule over most of what makes up present-day India. He then ruled for almost forty peaceful and prosperous years, during which time he had pillars erected all over his realm bearing carved inscriptions to proclaim his policies. He is also said to have redistributed the relics of the Buddha throughout the land, built 84,000 stupas to house them, and established 32 Buddhist pilgrimage sites by personally visiting them. In other words, he marked the Indian landscape as Buddhist, though he was a wise enough ruler not to antagonize other religious groups, who were allowed to continue their practices.

Asoka was also an enthusiastic missionary, sending his representatives to the far reaches of his own territory and beyond to foreign countries. Through these activities he redefined kingship, transforming it into a specifically Buddhist form that embodied the Buddhist ideal of the *cakravartin*. Asoka literally had conquered the world, but he ruled according to dharma, Buddhist thought. He was a *dharmaraja*, a king of dharma, who protected and spread Buddhism.

Another feature of Asoka's Buddhist kingship is that he purified monastic practice and settled doctrinal disputes. Traditionally, it is said that there were a series of Buddhist councils held in ancient India to settle monastic disputes about doctrine and discipline. Asoka is said to have presided over one such council; he decided which monks were right and expelled those he thought were wrong. This royal precedent was extremely important for the later development of Buddhism, especially in Southeast Asia, where kings consciously imitated Asoka.

Overall, royal support was essential for the successful spread of Buddhism, and the Buddha's birth as an Indian prince and the many tales about his past lives as a prince or king appealed to other rulers.

Theravada and Mahayana Buddhism

Various schools of Buddhism began to distinguish themselves soon after the death of the Buddha. This period of early Buddhism is best described as sectarian Buddhism, of which Theravada ("the way of the elders") is the only surviving school. Around the first century before the Common Era, another form of Buddhism, Mahayana ("the great vehicle"), began to take shape. For centuries, these two distinct but friendly schools of Buddhism successfully coexisted in monasteries, though they eventually expanded into different parts of Asia.

Theravada, or as it is sometimes called, southern Buddhism, spread south from northern India into Sri Lanka and eventually east to Myanmar, Thailand, Cambodia, and Laos. Its ideal type is the *arhat*, a nun or monk who has achieved enlightenment and therefore is believed not to reincarnate. By achieving enlightenment, *arhat*s duplicate the experience of the Buddha so they, too, are believed to remember their past lives and even to possess magical powers, such as the ability to read people's minds or to fly or walk on water. Such powers are believed to be by-products of intense meditation practice and not ends in themselves. So the rules for monastics forbid them to perform such feats in public. The term *arhat* is still used for such rare people in the southern schools of Buddhism.

Mahayana, or northern Buddhism, took shape as a separate school of Buddhism in northern India. It is the form of Buddhism that spread north to Tibet and east to China, Korea, and Japan. This school believes it teaches the private doctrines of the Buddha, his non-public teachings. Their sacred texts, called *sutra*s, usually begin with the phrase "Thus have I heard" and proceed to say that, while the Buddha was residing in such a place, he gave the following teaching. All Mahayana teachings refer to the historical Buddha or to divine buddhas. The religious ideal of Mahayana Buddhism is the bodhisattva, an enlightened being of infinite compassion who has made the vow to achieve buddhahood but who postpones final personal enlightenment so that she or he may continue to reincarnate in order to help all other beings to achieve enlightenment. Bodhisattvas can be female, male, divine, human, or animal. Their lives are devoted to relieving the suffering of all beings and helping them to reach buddhahood. It is also the term generally used for the Buddha before he achieved enlightenment. Particularly holy women and men living today are believed to be bodhisattvas.

Human bodhisattvas strive to perfect themselves through giving, developing patience, making an effort in whatever they do, practicing meditation, and developing their wisdom. The ideal examples of these activities are taken from the past-life stories of the Buddha. All of these *jataka*s are said to have been told by the Buddha. One of the most ancient collections of *jakata*s contains more than five hundred of his past lives. The most famous of these is that of Prince Vessantara, whose life exemplifies the virtue of giving. Vessantara gave whatever was asked of him. When he gave away the rare and famous white elephant that was believed to assure the prosperity of his country, he and his family were exiled to the forest. He and his wife, together with their small son and daughter, left the city in a chariot drawn by four horses, but he soon gave that away as well. They built huts in the forest and lived off the fruits they gathered. One day, however, a wanderer asked Vessantara for his two children, and Vessantara gave them to him. Then a priest asked for his wife, and Vessantara gave her away, too. The story is meant to show his bottomless generosity. It ends well, though, because his wife, children, and country were all restored to him. This particular *jataka* is enormously popular throughout Southeast Asia, where there are elaborate, ritualized preachings about it.

In another *jataka* the Buddha is a young man who comes upon a tigress that is too weak to hunt because she has just given birth. To feed her and ensure the safety of her cubs, the Buddha gave her his body to eat by throwing himself off a precipice.

Celestial bodhisattvas are divine beings who can be prayed to by human beings. One of the best known and most complex is Avalokitesvara. He is often shown with one thousand arms and with an eye of compassion in the palm of each of his one thousand hands. With these

compassion

Compassion is the main quality of all buddhas and bodhisattvas, whether human or divine. Their compassion is limitless and is extended to all animals and people, regardless of species or class, because buddhas and bodhisattvas have experienced the oneness of all beings. For them, there simply is no difference between one person and another, or between an animal and a person. It is an active virtue because they do or say things to lessen the suffering of others. They are guided by an enlightened wisdom that enables them to know the right thing to do or say. In this way, compassion is distinguished from pity, which is passive.

Avalokitesvara, of the many hands, is portrayed in this seventeenth-century Tibetan sculpture of bronze and semiprecious stones.

one thousand eyes, Avalokitesvara sees all the suffering beings throughout the world and is ready to aid them. He is the great protector from all kinds of physical danger. He is described in the *Lotus Sutra*, a Buddhist text composed by the early third century C.E. in India and later translated into most of the languages of Asia.

As the belief in Avalokitesvara spread throughout Asia, he was transformed into a female deity known as Kuan Yin in China and Kannon in Japan, and referred to as the goddess of mercy. In Tibet he remained male but is associated with Tara, a female celestial bodhisattva well known for her compassion and her ability to protect those who appeal to her from any danger. Avalokitesvara is the patron deity of Tibet. His mantra, or the holy syllables that invoke him, *om mani padme hum*, is endlessly recited by young and old, lay and monastic. Additionally, the Dalai Lamas, traditionally the spiritual and political leaders of Tibet, are believed to be incarnations of Avalokitesvara. This is a dramatic example of the belief that bodhisattvas, celestial and human, continue to reincarnate in order to help all beings to achieve enlightenment.

Mahayana is a widening of Buddhist doctrine based mainly on the worship of sacred literature; devotion to the buddhas of the past, present, and future; and prayer to celestial buddhas and bodhisattvas. From the earliest days of Buddhism, buddhas of the past were represented in art and literature. Gautama Buddha is the buddha of our eon, and other earlier eons had their buddhas as well. There is also a future buddha for the next eon, Maitreya, who sits in Tusita Heaven awaiting his time to incarnate. The sacred texts of Mahayana Buddhism are said to come from these divine buddhas and bodhisattvas and are treated as relics. The sacred writings themselves receive offerings of incense and are ritually circumambulated.

Mahayana emphasizes contemplation, visualization, and

most importantly recitations of the name of particular celestial buddhas, such as Amitabha. Reciting the name of a particular buddha had great appeal to laypeople who, for various reasons, could not or would not become monks or nuns. Celestial buddhas are believed to have achieved enlightenment many eons ago, long before the time of Gautama Buddha. They, too, were originally human bodhisattvas who, when they made their vows to become buddhas, described the Pure Land they would create. A Pure Land is a celestial realm where the teachings of a buddha hold sway. It is a heaven that has been purified by the presence and teachings of a buddha, in contrast to an impure land that lacks a buddha and his teachings.

The Pure Land of the buddha Amitabha is called Sukhavati, the Land of Bliss, also known as the Western Paradise. This is the Pure Land encountered most often in literature and art. Its name, *sukha* ("bliss"), sets up a contrast with *dukha* ("suffering"), the defining characteristic of cyclical existence with its inevitable round of being born, growing old, and dying followed by being born again. Sukhavati is depicted as a sweet-smelling and beautiful garden with lotus ponds and trees made of precious jewels, a place where the plants and birds preach the dharma and all the needs of its inhabitants are satisfied. Rebirth into Sukhavati can be achieved by a combination of good deeds and by repeating, in some cases by just hearing, the name of Amitabha Buddha. The simplicity of this practice, repeating Ambitabha's name, made it accessible to vast numbers of people who were illiterate or who could not pursue more time-consuming rituals. The recitation of his name could be done while working at other tasks, such as farming or housework, though ritualized recitation with a group of worshippers was also commonly practiced. Rebirth into this paradise is one's final incarnation, since it is inevitable that buddhahood will be achieved here. Pure Land Buddhism became an extremely popular and widespread form of worship through Asia.

Some Pure Lands are on earth. They are hidden lands, invisible to all but the most spiritually developed beings. Tibetan Buddhists believe in such a land, called Shambhala, which is said to be very beautiful, a land that is both within human experience and beyond it. It is envisioned as a fertile land of valleys and mountains hidden deep within several rings of snow-covered mountain ranges lying somewhere to the north of India. Eight regions surround the central capital, where the king—a benevolent and fully enlightened being—rules from a palace constructed of precious jewels. Its residents live in perfect harmony and happiness, since all their needs are met. Everyone has long, healthy lives but eventually they do die; most go on to enlightenment and others are reborn once again into Shambhala or into similar divine realms. The main activity in this kingdom is the pursuit of enlightenment. This is easily achieved in such an environment and through learning the teachings of the *Kalacakra Tantra* ("the wheel of time tantra"), a private teaching of the Buddha's said to have been taught by him and then preserved for centuries in Shambhala. Tibetans believe that initiation into the teachings of the *Kalacakra Tantra* assures rebirth into Shambhala.

Shambhala is also the focus of beliefs about the end of the world. An important prophecy about Shambhala is that during the reign of its twenty-fifth king, around the year 2425, an enormous war will engulf the whole world. At that time, just when all seems lost, a great army will march forth from Shambhala to conquer the opposing forces. Peace will be restored throughout the world, ushering in a golden age.

This Tibetan painting on paper shows the kingdom of Shambhala ringed by its eight surrounding regions. The king is portrayed holding court in the center.

Vajrayana Buddhism

A third school of Buddhism—variously called Vajrayana (the thunderbolt or diamond vehicle), Tantric, and Esoteric Buddhism—began to surface sometime around the fifth century C.E. Vajrayana had its roots in Mahayana Buddhism as well as ancient religious beliefs of northern India that included magical and shamanistic elements and the worship of goddesses. Shamanism often involves trancelike ritual journeys in which a ritual expert called a shaman meets and subdues gods and demons in order to gain their powers. All these elements were incorporated into tantric practices which spread throughout both the Buddhist and Hindu worlds.

Tantric, or Vajrayana, Buddhism stresses enlightenment in one lifetime through extreme practices involving individual visionary experiences, vivid sexual imagery, and the use of forbidden substances such as wine and meat in its rituals. Tantric practices often take place at night in cemeteries to avoid the prying eyes of the non-initiated and to conquer the fear of death. The chief practitioner of Tantric Buddhism is called a *siddha*, a wandering ascetic who is also a wonder-worker. There were, and are, women *siddhas*, but most often they are described as male.

Central to Tantric ritual are what are called the five *m*'s. In Sanskrit all of the words begin with *m*, but in English the words are *wine, meat, fish, parched grain*, and *sexual union*. The first four are said to arouse sexual desire and lead to the fifth: actual or symbolic sexual union. Theoretically, there are two forms of Tantric practice: the right-handed path, in which a person uses substitutes for the first four *m*'s and visualizes the fifth, sexual union; and the left-handed path, in which a person is said to actually eat and drink these substances and involves ritual sexual intercourse. Left-handed practice also

frequently uses substitutes and visualization. Generally, tantric monks maintained their vows of celibacy by using visualization in tantric rituals.

The five *m*'s are forbidden to Hindus because they are polluting, but the tantric practitioner, whether Buddhist or Hindu, ritually uses these forbidden substances to get beyond the concepts of good and evil, forbidden and allowed, and to achieve an experience of the ultimate union of all opposites, even of female and male. For instance, in Buddhism wisdom, *prajna*, is feminine and passive; although skillful means, *upaya*, is male and active. Joining these two through actual or symbolic sexual union leads to enlightenment. This combining of opposites is portrayed in Tantric Buddhist art and texts that show celestial bodhisattvas and buddhas with divine female

These Buddhist stupas and temples are found in what has now been designated an archaeological zone in Bagan, Myanmar.

wisdom

Wisdom, called *prajna*, is valued and sought after by all practitioners of Buddhism because it is an essential element of the enlightenment experience. *Prajna* received its fullest treatment in the earliest texts of Mahayana Buddhism, texts composed around the first century C.E. called *Prajnaparamita,* "The Perfection of Wisdom." As their name suggests, these works discuss the means of attaining or perfecting wisdom. Though wisdom is developed and grows through the continuing practice of the Buddhist virtues and meditation, one also needs to comprehend the concept of emptiness, the emptiness of all live beings and things. Emptiness completes the Buddhist's sense that the world is illusory. Dreams are frequently used to illustrate both emptiness and illusion. On awakening we are sometimes startled to find we were asleep and that our dream experience was an illusion. We realize that the dream was without substance, empty and void. In this sense, awakening from a dream is not just awakening *from* the state of illusion to that of reality, but rather it is an awakening *to* the unreality, the emptiness of both states, because waking reality is believed to be as insubstantial, as empty, as a dream. Awakening from a dream can provide a suggestion of enlightenment itself. It is the achievement of wisdom that enables the bodhisattva to maintain enlightened consciousness while aiding those whose consciousness is bound by the illusions of worldly reality.

Prajna, or wisdom, is often represented as a goddess and is frequently called "the Mother of all the Buddhas," because enlightenment is born from wisdom, as in the following description:

> I pay homage to the perfection of wisdom! She is worthy of homage. She is unstained, and the entire world cannot stain her. She is a source of light, and from everyone in the triple world she removes darkness, and leads them away from the blinding darkness caused by defilements and wrong views. In her we can find shelter. Most excellent are her works. She makes us seek the safety of the wings of enlightenment. She brings light to the blind, so that all fear and distress may be forsaken.

consorts called *prajnas*, female wisdom beings. A celestial buddha embracing his consort is understood to represent the mystical union of wisdom with skillful means. A symbolic enactment of this idea occurs when tantric monks manipulate two instruments while performing a ritual. In their left hands they hold a bell, a feminine symbol for wisdom; while in their right hands they manipulate a *vajra*, a thunderbolt, a masculine symbol for skillful means. The practitioner's goal is to merge with the celestial buddhas and their consorts, to actually become a buddha. In this respect Tantra stresses the ability of human beings to become divine beings like buddhas.

Tantric texts and practices are purposely difficult to understand because these teachings are supposed to be kept secret. They require complete dependence on a guru, a spiritual teacher, for preliminary training followed by initiation. Without initiation and instruction, the texts remain obscure and the rituals unknowable. In Tantric Buddhism the line of direct instruction and initiation usually goes back to a celestial buddha who is believed to have transmitted the teaching to a human being, who in turn passed it on to his disciple, and so on, down through the centuries. Tantric rituals are believed to contact powerful and dangerous forces, so one must be confident that the instruction received originated with an even more powerful divine source. Typically, the guru gives the student a mantra, syllables and Sanskrit words that confer power over various deities or are used to invoke celestial buddhas and bodhisattvas. Since visualization is also an important part of tantric practice, there is a rich legacy of tantric art focused on the geometrical design of the *mandala*, a word that means

A mandala painted with powder for a special ceremony.

"circle." The basic form of a mandala is a circle enclosed in a square which is enclosed in an outer circle.

Tantric Buddhism spread throughout south, southeastern, central, and east Asia and survives today among Buddhists in the Himalayan countries of Tibet, Nepal, and Bhutan; among the Shingon and Tendai Buddhists in Japan; and among exiled Tibetans everywhere. Not all Tantric Buddhists participate in these

Mandalas

Mandalas are graphic representations of the whole of reality and are important parts of Buddhist initiation rituals. They can be either temporary constructions or more lasting works of art. Temporary mandalas are drawn on the ground with chalk, powder, or string, to mark off the ritual area from the mundane world. Drawing or laying out the mandala is the beginning of the rituals that call various supernatural beings and powers into the mandala. The guru prepares the initiate by having him or her memorize and visualize all aspects of the mandala and by teaching mantras to activate their powers. During the initiation ceremony, the student symbolically enters the mandala, sometimes by tossing a flower into it, and takes on the powers of the gods located in it by envisioning all its details and by reciting mantras accompanied by ritual hand gestures (mudras) or the manipulation of ritual objects. In these ways, the body, mind, and speech of the initiate are all fully engaged by gesturing, visualizing, and saying the mantras. When the initiate's identification with the central deity of the mandala is complete, her or his sense of personal individuality is put aside, and the concept of duality—that there is a "you" and a "me"—dissolves. Within the mandala there is only the complete union of initiate and deity. At the end of the ritual, mandalas that were drawn on the ground are respectfully taken apart and disposed of in a river.

esoteric rituals which may take years of preparation. Laypeople and many monks and nuns are content with less complicated practices like circumambulating sacred structures, going on pilgrimages, chanting, and performing meritorious acts.

three

THE SPREAD OF BUDDHISM IN ASIA

Buddhism gradually spread to other countries through the conscious effort of missionary monks, the continual presence of traveling Buddhist merchants along lucrative trade routes, and royal support. Buddhist kings often used their influence with other, non-Buddhist kings, to encourage Buddhism. Once a king was converted, the rest of the country usually followed his example. Buddhism was very successful in adapting itself to many diverse cultures, in part because it incorporated local religious practices, rather than opposing them. This meant that wherever Buddhism reached, it maintained a core of beliefs, yet it also took on the flavors of many different countries, which emphasized different aspects of Buddhism. In fact, Buddhism was the first world religion.

Theravada Buddhism

Emperor Asoka, who supported the spread of Buddhism in India, also sent Buddhist missionaries to other countries. According to the ancient Sri Lankan chronicle, the *Mahavamsa,* around the year 250 B.C.E. Asoka sent his son Mahinda to Sri Lanka to convert the people there. Mahinda, who lived about 282–222 B.C.E., had become a Buddhist monk. He began by teaching King Devanampiyatissa, who was eager to meet the son of as famous a king as Asoka. Devanampiyatissa immediately converted to Buddhism, as did the rest of his court. Many men were ordained. For the ordination of nuns, Asoka's daughter—the nun Sanghamitta—had to be invited to Sri Lanka. She brought with her a sapling from the Bo Tree at Bodh Gaya, which she planted. This symbolically and quite concretely established the Buddha's teaching in the kingdom. To this day it is said that the tree she planted at Anuradhapura still flourishes, and it is the focus of intense devotion.

With the conversion of the Sri Lankan king, Buddhism became the state religion. However, another Indian religion also spread to Sri Lanka and other parts of Southeast Asia: the early form of Hinduism known as Brahmanism. So, alongside Buddhist practices and monasteries, Hindu practices and temples also flourished. And all of Southeast Asia had native forms of religion involving spirit worship, shamanism, and animism.

Buddhist policy was not to interfere very much with local religions. Buddhists accept the existence of gods, but believe that the gods cannot help a person achieve enlightenment. Despite this limitation, Buddhists accept that gods and spirits can be helpful in worldly matters. So, native religious ideas and practices tended to mingle with Buddhism, creating a different kind of Buddhism in each country. Today Sri Lanka and all the countries of Southeast Asia practice Theravada Buddhism, but Theravada has developed differently in each country.

The spread of Buddhism to Myanmar is a case in point. Starting in the third century B.C.E., Indian merchants brought different Buddhist schools to the region. Eventually, varieties of Theravada, Mahayana, and Vajrayana Buddhism all flourished there until the eleventh century C.E., when Theravada became the state religion. Similarly, during the first century C.E. Buddhist traders brought different varieties of Buddhism to Cambodia.

In Sri Lanka, though, many of the learned monks disapproved of non-Buddhist religious influences and wanted a purer form of Buddhist practice. The continued search for the pure Buddhism of the Buddha has shaped the history and practice of Sri Lankan Buddhism. Since the Buddhist tradition allows the king authority in matters of monastic doctrine and discipline, the history of Buddhism in Sri Lanka is one of kings ordering the monks to reform themselves and of monks seeking royal support for the reforms they wanted to institute.

In Sri Lanka as elsewhere, the teachings of the Buddha and the commentaries about them were originally preserved orally. Individual monks memorized different parts of the teachings and the commentaries and recited them when asked. Given the frequency of invasions, famines, and other disasters, some monks decided that this was too risky a way to transmit the precious words. The death of a monk who had memorized a particular teaching before he had taught it to another would mean its permanent loss. So it was arranged that Buddhist doctrine be written down. This became the multivolume Pali Canon; Pali was an ancient Indian language. This tendency to gather and standardize Buddhist texts continued as Buddhism spread throughout Asia, and is the reason there are the several Buddhist canons that exist today. These canons contain many similar sections like lengthy rules for monks and nuns, as well as writings from later periods.

The fears of the Buddhist monks in Sri Lanka eventually proved true. In 1017 the great Buddhist center of Anuradhapurna fell into the hands of invading Tamil Hindu forces, and the Buddhist king was defeated. Both orders of Buddhist monks and nuns, no longer the recipients of royal support and armed protection, were stamped out on the island—after enduring fifty years of political chaos and marauding troops. Fortunately for Buddhism, most of present-day Myanmar had been brought under the control of King Anawrahta who ruled from 1040 to 1077. He was an enthusiastic champion of Theravada Buddhism. In 1065 he received a request from the new Buddhist king of Sri Lanka for help in re-establishing the Buddhist order of monks. Buddhism requires that at least five monks must be present for anyone to receive full ordination. This request shows that monastic Buddhism had been so undermined by war and political chaos, that five fully ordained monks could not be found on the entire island of Sri Lanka. King Anawrahta therefore sent a group of monks to Sri Lanka.

However, there was no request to restore the order of Buddhist nuns, which required the presence of both ordained monks and nuns. As a consequence, their order was not revived in Sri Lanka. It also died out in Myanmar after its capital was attacked by the Mongols in 1287. Today in Sri Lanka and Southeast Asia there are communities of Buddhist women referred to as eight- or ten-precept nuns. These are women who take the precepts of an ordained monk without an ordination ceremony. They dress in white, as opposed to the yellow or orange robes of the monks, and most often act as servants to the monks, though some choose to live independently and pursue good works and meditation.

From the eleventh century onward, Theravada Buddhism swept through Southeast Asia, where it became the state religion of Cambodia in the twelfth century, of Thailand in the thirteenth, and of Laos in the fourteenth. Southeast Asian kings modeled themselves on Emperor Asoka. Like him, they acted as *dharmaraja*s, as kings of dharma and therefore guardians of Buddhism. They also knew that state-controlled Buddhism was an excellent means of maintaining the stability of the society. Making Theravada Buddhism the state religion

Turning the wheel of dharma refers to the Buddha's first sermon, which is often depicted by an eight-spoke wheel, representing the Eightfold Path, and two kneeling deer on either side of it, representing the Deer Park. The wheel also recalls the Buddha's role as a *cakravartin*, the wheel turner or world conqueror. This particular representation is found in Tibet's Jokhang Monstery.

brought together the powerful institutions of kingship and religious life. One result of this was that other forms of Buddhism—like Mahayana and Vajrayana—gradually were suppressed.

The State and Religion

Buddhist kings are referred to as *dharmaraja*s, whose duty (dharma) is to protect and promote Buddhism (the Dharma) and to maintain order within the state and the monastic orders so that Buddhism can flourish. This reveals the two levels of dharma: the universal teachings of the Buddha, for the most part in the hands of monastics; and the particular duty of the king to maintain order in the world. Visually, both dharmas are represented by the *cakra* ("wheel"), which has been incorporated into royal insignia, and is everywhere in Buddhist art and literature. The Buddha is said to have turned the wheel of dharma when he first taught his five disciples. The Buddha is called *the* King of Dharma, the great expounder of dharma, which identifies the Buddha with kings and kingship and also plays on the Buddha's royal heritage—the king who chose dharma as his kingdom. All this echoes the double meaning of *cakravartin*—a great king or great ascetic—since all *cakravartin*s, in both the spiritual and earthly realms, are *dharmaraja*s.

In Southeast Asia, the Buddha is believed to be present through his relics and images, which make the land sacred and are also the source of political power. It takes a king, though, a *dharmaraja*, to actualize this power in the world. Great monastic institutions flourished with the support of the king, and in turn they were loyal to the king. Ideally, each sustains the activities of the other.

Further ways in which Buddhism complements royal power can be seen in the frequent depictions of celestial bodhisattvas as princes adorned with royal ornaments. First, this recalls the early life of the Buddha, when he was a bodhisattva and a prince. Second, when Buddhism spread throughout Asia, many rulers had themselves painted and sculpted as celestial bodhisattvas. They presented themselves as being incarnated on earth for the purpose of leading their people to enlightenment by providing a stable society in which Buddhist teachings could flourish. Such kings built enduring monuments that link royal power and Buddhism. For example, King Jayavarman VII of Cambodia, who ruled from 1181 to about 1219, constructed a grand temple to the celestial bodhisattva Avalokitesvara and put his own face on the main image of Avalokitesvara as well as on those on its towers. Of course, some of this overlapping is due to ancient pre-Buddhist beliefs that kings were divine beings.

The period of Theravada Buddhism expansion came to an end in the sixteenth century, when Buddhism began a period of decline under European colonial rule.

Throughout Southeast Asia there have always been two dominant types of monks: forest monks and village monks. As these terms indicate, one kind of monk lives away from society, deep in the forest, while the other lives in villages and is involved with the laity. The forest monks live apart from the distractions of daily life so they may pursue study and meditation. Forest monks have their lay supporters, some of whom they guide in meditation and other Buddhist practices. In contrast to this austere life, village monks participate in the goings-on of their village, perform ceremonies to benefit the laity, and function as centers of Buddhist knowledge. Since there is so much activity at village monasteries, the monks have little time for meditation.

Both types of monks are, for the laity, sources of merit, which they obtain by supporting the monastic community, listening to their sermons, chanting prayers with them in Pali, and learning meditation. The mutual benefit that village monks and the laity can receive from each other can be seen in a typical merit-making ceremony of Thai Buddhism. It is performed on mornings of the full, new, and half moons. Simply put, in this ritual the villagers exchange food for merit. When looked at more closely, though, complexities become apparent. Before donating the food, the villagers first honor the main statue of Buddha and reaffirm their commitment to Buddhism by taking refuge in the Three Jewels and accepting the five precepts of moral behavior from the chief monk. One gains more merit by living according to the five precepts, yet problems arise during daily life that make the precepts hard to follow. Ritually re-accepting the five precepts puts the villagers

This young Thai novice is given early exposure to the life of a monk.

in a purer state—at least as long as the ritual lasts. The villagers then formally say what they are donating, specifically mentioning the benefits they hope to gain, and conclude with the wish that the donation will someday lead to their enlightenment. Then the food is given to the monks, who chant over it and eat it. When the monks' meal is finished, one monk delivers a sermon, after which the villagers have their meal.

Additionally, many boys undergo temporary ordinations, which is another source of merit. In Thailand almost every man has been a monk, if only for a few weeks. In part this is because monasteries are also educational institutions, especially for the poor. Frequently, though, when a parent becomes ill, her or his child may vow to become a monk for a certain period of time if the parent becomes well again. These exchanges reveal merit as a source of power that can be put to other uses, either for oneself or for others.

Mahayana Buddhism

Mahayana Buddhists were no less enthusiastic than Theravada Buddhists in their missionary activity. Although their teachings spread into Sri Lanka and Southeast Asia, they were driven out by the success of Theravada Buddhism and the tendency of kings to eliminate other forms of Buddhism. In the north, though, Mahayana Buddhism met with enormous success. Here again, Buddhism was spread by three primary means: missionizing monks, Buddhist traders who ventured far from home in search of markets, and royal support. And, as in Southeast Asia, Mahayana Buddhism incorporated local religious practices and created equally distinct forms of Buddhism in each country.

The Silk Road

In about the first century B.C.E., nomads conquered large parts of Afghanistan, northern India, and central Asia. This was the beginning of the Kushan empire; and one of its kings, Kanishka I, converted to Buddhism. In addition to whatever personal satisfaction Kanishka found in Buddhism, the religion proved useful for uniting his widespread and religiously diverse realm.

The Kushan empire lasted until the third century C.E., providing centuries of political and military stability along one of the world's important trade routes: the Silk Road, named after the valuable cloth that was traded along its length. Monks and merchants followed this route, spreading Buddhism throughout the region and into China.

When the Kushan empire collapsed in the third century C.E., the activity along the Silk Road continued without interruption—traffic even increased. Kingdoms formed around the central Asian cities, and once again kings and rich merchants showed their support for Buddhism by building beautiful temples, commissioning works of art, supporting monasteries, and translating Buddhist texts into the languages of central and east Asia. When Buddhism spread into China, Chinese pilgrim-monks began traveling the road westward, back to India, to study Buddhism in its homeland. One of the earliest such monks was Fa-hsien, who spent fifteen years traveling and studying (399–414 C.E.). He wrote a brief account of his journey in which he described his stay in Khotan, a city-state southwest of the Gobi Desert. He said Khotan "is a pleasant and prosperous kingdom, with a numerous and flourishing population. The inhabitants all profess our Law [dharma]. . . . There are countless numbers of monks, most of whom are students of the Mahayana."

Fa-hsien stayed for three months in one of Khotan's monasteries which alone housed three thousand monks and where he witnessed the annual procession of the main statue of Buddha. This ceremony began by sweeping all the streets of the city clean and pouring water over them. The great cart that carried the Buddha image was richly decorated with jewels and silk, and the king and queen publicly paid their respects to it at the city gate. Fa-hsien described the scene:

> **When (the cart) was a hundred paces from the gate, the king put off his crown of state, changed his dress for a fresh suit, and with bare feet, carrying in his hands flowers and incense, and with two rows of attending followers, went out at the gate to meet the image; and, with his head and face (bowed to the ground), he did homage at its feet, and then scattered the flowers and burnt the incense. When the image was entering the gate, the queen and the brilliant ladies with her in the gallery above scattered far and wide all kinds of flowers. . . .**

Fa-hsien's description is a wonderful record of royal devotion to Buddhism and the active participation of royalty in its public rituals.

Between the seventh and ninth centuries, Tibet conquered extensive parts of this region, won control of the Silk Road, and gradually was converted to Buddhism. Soon after the collapse of the Tibetan empire in the ninth century, Islam became the dominant religion of the region, but the Muslims could not withstand the conquering Mongols under Genghis Khan (about 1162–1227), who destroyed whatever religious culture they found, although Kublai Khan (1215–1294) became known for his religious tolerance. Several cities along the Silk Road were abandoned and slipped back into the desert, not to be rediscovered until the twentieth century. But, by that time, Buddhism had long taken root in China.

china

When Buddhism reached China in the first century C.E., China had one of the most complex and sophisticated cultures in Asia. The Chinese thought of themselves as the only civilized people in the world. They had a complicated social organization and the long-standing native religious traditions of Confucianism and Taoism, as well as a vital spiritualism. For these reasons, they were not at first particularly receptive to a foreign religion.

Taoism and confucianism

Confucianism began in the works of its founder, Confucius (551–479 B.C.E.), especially the *Analects*, a collection of Confucius's conversations with his pupils and his advice to rulers. Additionally, Confucius took as authoritative the texts of ancient China, such as the *Book of Changes*. Together, these texts are referred to as the Confucian Classics and are considered by Confucians to be the source of all wisdom.

The underlying idea of these works is that the cosmos is orderly because it is based on relationships that are hierarchical and harmonious. In Confucius's attempt to duplicate this order in earthly matters, he emphasized three things: relationship, hierarchy, and harmony. These are best understood in the relationship between heaven and earth in which heaven, a male principle, is thought of as dominating and sustaining the earth, a female principle. The hierarchy in this relationship is clear: heaven dominates the earth. Yet the harmony and balance of the relationship is revealed by the orderly course of nature. In human terms, this pattern is expressed primarily through the ideal Confucian family in which the husband rules over the wife, the father over the son. The model of the family is repeated in the Confucian state in which the emperor rules over everyone. This idea received additional expression in the concept of two principles that exist in all things. Called yin and yang, these principles can be thought of as passive female qualities or active male ones. For example, individual women and men contain yin and yang qualities in their characters and bodies, and good health and tranquillity are believed to spring from the harmonious blending of the two.

The semilegendary figure of Lao Tzu is traditionally credited with the founding of Taoism in the sixth century B.C.E. According to this tradition, Lao Tzu decided to seek the life of a recluse far from the paths of civilization. On his way out of the city, a gatekeeper asked him to share his wisdom, and Lao Tzu agreed to do this by composing the *Tao Te Ching* and leaving it with the guard.

This text is rich in paradox and mystical insight. It accepts Chinese cosmological beliefs like the harmonious nature of the cosmos and the relationship of yin and yang. In general, the work recommends that individuals model themselves after nature, which demonstrates this cosmic harmony, and pursue a passive quietism and mystical union with the Tao (understood to be the source of all being). Much of the text is directed to political leaders, who are advised to become sages, to rule without force, to be passive, and to harmonize their natures with the Tao. If they do this, then the people will automatically submit to their rulers. At the same time, the *Tao Te Ching* also lends itself to the ideal of the sage as a recluse, someone who has left society to pursue self-cultivation in harmony with nature.

In addition to its foreignness, the Chinese had other objections to Buddhism. Its ascetic practices, such as fasting and shaving the head, and the practice of cremating the dead went against the Chinese view of the body as a gift from one's parents that had to be well taken care of. A central Chinese virtue is that of filial piety: the duty children owe their parents. The monastic Buddhist practice of abandoning home and family clashed with these Chinese values and social organization. Connected to filial piety is the important role of ancestor worship, which requires people to marry and have children, not to become celibate monastics. The Buddhists had various responses to this criticism. For example, they argued that they performed the highest filial piety by leading their parents to Buddhism and thus ensuring their salvation. This point is dramatically made in an ancient Chinese legend.

Once there was a king with three daughters. The older two were married, but the youngest, Miao-shan, wanted to be a Buddhist nun and refused to marry. Her father had her punished, but she escaped into the mountains where she built a small hut, wore clothes made of grass, and ate fruit from trees. A few years went by, and the king became very ill and none of the doctors could cure him. A strange monk went to the king and said he knew of a magic remedy: a medicine made from the eyes and arms of someone free from all anger. The king said that would be hard to find, but the monk told him a holy woman living on a mountain would give these parts of her body if the king asked. The king sent a messenger to make the request and to say such a gift "[would] lead him to turn his mind to enlightenment." Without hesitation, Miao-shan gouged out her eyes and cut off both her arms. At that moment the whole earth shook—a sign of the great merit of her gift. When the king was better, he went to the mountain to offer his thanks and venerate the holy woman. He saw her without eyes or arms, but even so she reminded him of his lost daughter. The woman acknowledged that she was Miao-shan, saying, "Your daughter has offered her arms and eyes to repay her father's love." The king wept and bemoaned making his daughter suffer. Miao-shan said she was not in pain, and then heaven and earth shook as she was revealed to be the all-merciful celestial bodhisattva Kuan Yin, a female version of Avalokitesvara.

Although Miao-shan is initially unfilial in disobeying her father's wish that she marry, in the end she is the most filial of children. She sacrifices even her eyes and arms for her father's health and for his spiritual advancement; it is through her sacrifice that he comes to accept the Buddhist path and experiences the compassion that leads to his salvation.

A related story, that of Mu-lien, a Buddhist filial son, became an important ritual and an opera in China, which indicates how important it was to include filial piety in Buddhist ritual. As mentioned earlier, the wheel of rebirth includes the realm of hungry ghosts, beings who are unable to satisfy their huge appetites and thirsts because their necks are as thin as needles and so nothing can pass through them. The story of Mu-lien came from an Indian tale in which one of the Buddha's disciples, Maudgalyayana (*Mu-lien* in Chinese and *Murkuren* in Japanese), visits his mother in heaven. In the Chinese and Japanese versions the visit takes place in hell, where Mu-lien is unsuccessful in attempting to relieve the suffering of his mother. He returns to the land of the living to seek advice from the Buddha, who tells him his mother's suffering could be relieved if he provided food and cloth offerings to monastics. Mu-lien does as he is told, and his mother is saved from hell. This story is a model for later Buddhists to follow if they want to save their ancestors, because the merit acquired by making food offerings to monastics could be transferred to one's dead relatives.

Even though Buddhism was adjusted to accommodate Chinese values, it faced an additional problem because it came to China in bits and pieces. Individual travelers, merchants, and monks—either Theravada or Mahayana Buddhists—arrived with their texts and teachings, as did central Asian monks with still other Buddhist writings and Buddhist merchants with domestic practices. This meant there was no coherent system of Buddhism, which was also the case as Buddhism spread into Southeast and central Asia. As foreign monks continued to migrate to China, bringing new texts with them, the dharma became increasingly contradictory. An important part of the Chinese Buddhist reaction to this was for Chinese monks, such as Fa-hsien, to make the long journey to India to study Buddhism in its homeland.

Despite these problems, Buddhist monasticism became established in China. As early as 317, Chu Ching-chien (about 292–361) became the first Chinese Buddhist nun and founded a convent in the capital of Ch'ang-an. Full ordination for nuns was not established until 434, when a group of Sri Lankan nuns arrived in China for that purpose. Eventually, there were three types of Buddhist monastics in China: village and forest monastics similar to those in Southeast Asia, and large monasteries patronized and often controlled by the ruling elite.

Among the Buddhist teachings that became popular with monastics and the laity were devotional cults, especially those centered on the celestial buddha Amitabha and the female celestial bodhisattva Kuan Yin. The worship of Kuan Yin began in India as the worship of the male celestial bodhisattva Avalokitesvara. A chapter in the *Lotus Sutra* describes Avalokitesvara's protective powers.

> **If a man given up to capital punishment implores Avalokitesvara, the swords of the executioners shall snap asunder. Further, if the whole universe were teeming with goblins and giants, they would by virtue of pronouncing the name of Avalokitesvara lose the faculty of sight. If some creature is bound in wooden or iron manacles, chains or fetters, be he guilty or innocent, then those manacles, chains or fetters shall give way as soon as the name of Avalokitesvara is pronounced. Such is the power of the bodhisattva Avalokitesvara.**

In terms of gender, the *Lotus Sutra* described the different forms Avalokitesvara took when he preached in various worlds. For instance, he could appear as a buddha, a bodhisattva, one of the gods, or a man. In the original Indian text, all the forms are male. However, when the text was translated into Chinese in the early fifth century, it included female forms such as a nun, a woman, and a wife. The inclusion of female forms in the *Lotus Sutra* and the popularity of Miao-shan and stories in which Kuan Yin appears as a young woman all contributed to a gradual shift to female forms in Chinese Buddhism during the tenth century, though male images of Kuan Yin also continued to be produced.

In 581 Emperor Wen-ti, who ruled from 581 to 604, was able to unite China, in part through his policy of promoting Buddhism combined with Confucianism. Royal support of Chinese Buddhism led to translations of Buddhist texts and the establishment of great monasteries. Over the centuries, however, relations between Buddhism and the royal family fluctuated. Some Buddhist emperors lavished donations on monasteries and temples, which later, non-Buddhist emperors would stop.

A difficult period for Buddhism lasted from 842 until 845, when a government-organized persecution destroyed monasteries, temples, and shrines across the empire and forced more than 200,000 monks and nuns to return to lay life. This disaster was added to later by the Huang Ch'ao Rebellion (875–884), which, although political in nature, had as a side effect the destruction of many monasteries. In the end, the Buddhist teachings that survived in China were centered on neither imperial power nor the scholastic tradition supported by the monastic libraries. One school that continued was the iconoclastic Ch'an or meditation Buddhism. The ideal practitioner of Ch'an (called Zen in Japan and Son in Korea) was the spontaneous master, who lived beyond the norms of social convention, somewhat like the *siddha*s of Vajrayana Buddhism.

Although all forms of Buddhism emphasize meditation, it is the main practice of Ch'an, especially in the early stages of a disciple's training. Through meditation, the Ch'an practitioner comes to understand reality, to move beyond the idea of duality—of you and me—and instead to grasp the oneness of everyone and everything. Ch'an practitioners say that enlightenment occurs when the mind is in a spontaneous, nonverbal state generated by meditation. Toward this end, disciples gather around an enlightened master or guru and practice meditation for long hours each day, sometimes for many years. They try to maintain the meditative state even as they go about their daily routines. Indeed, field or kitchen work is part of this training.

Ch'an places a great emphasis on the guru who guides and tests the awareness of each disciple. Since he is already enlightened, the guru knows when the disciple is ready to be awakened. Instruction is conducted in a process referred to as mind-to-mind teachings, direct teachings from the guru's mind to the disciple's—without any word being spoken. Occasionally, a shout is enough, or a slap. For other students, it is a gesture that liberates them.

A dialogue, best known as the Japanese word *koan* (in Chinese: *kung-an*, in Korean: *kongan*) is used for its ability to confound ordinary rational or habitual processes. The guru would assign a koan to a disciple, such as asking, "What is the sound of one hand clapping?" Then the disciple would spend months, perhaps years, meditating on its meaning. In between, he or she would be called before the guru who would sternly repeat the question. The wrong answer, an answer that indicated that enlightenment had not yet been realized, would prompt the guru to shout at or even to hit the disciple, often driving him or her out of the meeting room. The difficulty of the koan lies in it having no right answer, just an answer that expresses a leap of comprehension to enlightened awareness.

Another popular form of Buddhism in China was the cult of Pure Lands and the celestial buddhas who created them, especially Amitabha Buddha, called Amitofo in China and Amida in Japan. While Ch'an requires effort and sustained practice to achieve the goal of enlightenment, the cult of Amitabha Buddha is more accessible to ordinary people because only devotion is required to reach its goal of rebirth in Amitabha's paradise. Devotion to Amitabha means endlessly reciting his name, which anyone can do whether he or she is farming

The Laughing Buddha

The image of the Laughing, or Mi-lo, Buddha is connected to Ch'an. This is a form of the future buddha Maitreya, who is said to have incarnated as the laughing fool Pu Tai, to whom obscure Ch'an sayings are attributed. He is usually shown sitting with his right leg partly raised, a fat naked belly, a wrinkled forehead, and a broad smile. His fat belly is an indication of his wealth, which means he is able to grant wealth to his devotees, while his smile and relaxed posture display his serenity and contentment. At other times he is standing with both hands raised straight up over his head. Originally, Maitreya was portrayed as a majestic young prince, but in Chinese court circles Amitabha became more popular. Around the tenth century, Mi-lo Buddha surfaced as an important folk deity in this fat, laughing form. Maitreya may appear on earth at any time, but mainly he waits in Tusita heaven for his time to incarnate on earth as the Buddha of the next eon.

or doing housework. The broad acceptance of reciting Amitabha's name was aided by the Indian belief that after the death of Gautama Buddha there would be three periods during which the dharma, the doctrines taught by the Buddha, would change. True Dharma would flourish for five hundred years after the Buddha lived; Counterfeit Dharma would follow and last for five hundred to one thousand years, depending on the tradition; and Degenerated Dharma would establish itself from then on. Degenerated Dharma was imagined to be a period of decline, at the end of which the future buddha Maitreya would descend to earth to teach the dharma. The Chinese of the sixth century thought the Buddha had lived in the tenth century B.C.E., and so, they saw themselves as living in the period of Degenerated Dharma, a time when easier practices, like reciting Amitabha's name, was sufficient.

Both Pure Land and Ch'an Buddhism taught that all beings already possess buddha nature, or full awareness—they only need to realize it. For Pure Land practitioners, buddha nature is realized by devotion to Amitabha Buddha. For Ch'an practitioners, the realization of buddha nature comes through meditation.

The Laughing Buddha has become a common iconic representation of the buddha and deity of prosperity.

Neither Pure Land nor Ch'an Buddhism promoted the building of a strong nation, although some of their practitioners and patrons were courtiers. Buddhism, therefore, became somewhat marginalized in China. Ch'an was more commonly practiced away from commercial and political centers, while Pure Land was popular with the vast laboring class. This changed somewhat in the Sung Dynasty (960–1279), when the government standardized discipline in the monasteries and controlled who could be ordained. As part of the government's program of standardization it financed the first printing of the Chinese Buddhist Canon. The printing took eleven years to complete and involved carving 130,000 wooden printing blocks. The Chinese Buddhist Canon is similar to the Pali Canon compiled in Sri Lanka, except that it also contains Mahayana texts.

Korea and Vietnam

Korea and Vietnam have been enormously influenced by the culture of China. Both countries adopted the Chinese form of writing and absorbed the Confucian philosophy that shaped their centralized government bureaucracies. At the same time, the Koreans and the Vietnamese wanted to maintain their own identity. Buddhism enabled them to do this because the ruling families in Korea and Vietnam saw Buddhism as an Indian, not a Chinese, religion. Indeed, Korean Buddhists believed that the Buddha had incarnated in Korea in a past life. In time, the Koreans came to see Buddhism as a vehicle for nationalist opposition to foreign military and cultural incursions. Nonetheless, Chinese forms of Buddhism—Ch'an, Pure Land, and the cult of Kuan Yin—became widespread in Korea and Vietnam.

Buddhism entered Korea through the royal courts. The kings saw that Buddhism could unify the diverse religious practices of the people they ruled. When Korea was unified by the Silla dynasty (668–935) in the seventh century, Buddhism became the state religion—but it was a Buddhism combined with Confucianism, Taoism, and native practices.

Devotion to the future buddha Maitreya was widespread. Images showed him as a handsome prince wearing a crown and jewels, sitting on his throne in Tusita heaven, waiting to be reborn on earth and become the buddha of that age. Korean kings justified their rule by portraying themselves as incarnations of Maitreya. This practice had its roots in the Buddhist idea of the *dharmaraja*. By portraying themselves as Maitreya's incarnations, Korean kings were not only representing themselves as the protectors and supporters of the dharma, they were also preparing the way for the future buddha.

In Korea, Ch'an Buddhism, called Son, emphasized scholarship along with meditation. Large groups of scholar-monks lived in monastic estates supported by the king. Due to the efforts of well-trained Korean monks throughout the centuries, Buddhist texts were translated and preserved. Many of the texts that had been lost in China during periods of persecution and political upheaval were later replaced by those preserved in Korean monastic libraries. With royal support, the Korean Buddhist Canon was carved on wooden printing blocks. The Korean Buddhist Canon is the equivalent of the Pali Canon of Theravada Buddhism with the addition of Mahayana and Vajrayana texts translated from Sanskrit and Chinese. Today the Korean Buddhist Canon remains a major source for Buddhism scholars.

The religious climate in Korea changed under the Yi dynasty (1392–1910), which made Confucianism the state religion and led to a decline of Buddhism. Eventually, Buddhism was persecuted outright: lands were confiscated, images were melted down, and monks were pressured to return to lay life. Similarly, in Vietnam Buddhism declined somewhat in the fifteenth century once Confucianism dominated the royal court.

Japan

In 552 King Syong-myong of Korea sent a gift of Buddhist statutes and texts to the Japanese imperial court. Like a *dharmaraja*, he was spreading Buddhism, but his other purpose was to win Japanese support for his military campaigns. The Japanese already had a religious system based on *kami*—sacred beings, objects, and places that were believed to possess spiritual power. Some *kami* were the spirit of Japan itself and therefore were protectors of the island kingdom. The basic political unit of pre-Buddhist Japan was the clan, each of which had its own *kami*, or protective spirit. So worship of the *kami* smoothly blended religious practice and political identity. Japanese rulers saw in Buddhism an opportunity to unite all the clans under imperial authority, and Prince Shotoku (573–621) became the most influential force in establishing Buddhism as the state religion. He was regent for his aunt, Empress Suiko, who ruled from 592 to 628 and wielded enormous power. He invited Korean monks and nuns to Japan—as well as Korean artisans—to build temples, and he sent Japanese monks and nuns to Korea for further study. His influence on Buddhism was so important that he was thought to be a bodhisattva who incarnated to save the Japanese people.

Korea had adopted Chinese script along with Buddhism, which meant that many of the Buddhist texts studied in Japan were in Chinese. The Japanese decided it would be better to have direct contact with Chinese teachers, so Prince Shotoku took the first step by opening diplomatic relations with the Chinese court. Under the influence of China, Confucianism was also incorporated into Japanese Buddhist practice, as was the worship of *kami*.

Buddhist nuns and monks continued to live near the royal court and to be involved in its religious and secular activities. This intimate mingling of court and monastic life, however, corrupted the monasteries. The imperial government had decreed that a certain number of monks had to be ordained every year. Because of that, many monks had no religious calling at all and continued to behave like laymen while living in the monasteries. They were ambitious for royal favors and maintained sexual relations with the women of the court. The Japanese imperial court seethed with intrigue, and many monks were in the thick of it.

Buddhism had little effect on the general population until the early ninth century, when individual monks with deep religious feelings separated from court life, established monastic centers far from the royal capital, and began to attract followers. The monk Kukai (774–835) made the journey to China to study Buddhism and brought Tantric Buddhism back to Japan. He called his teaching Shingon. He established a monastic center on Mount Koya where he insisted on strict monastic discipline and taught his disciples to recite mantras and visualize mandalas that would lead them to identify with and realize the total harmony of the universe. This monastery was closed to women.

Another monk, Saicho (767–822), established a monastery on Mount Hiei that also strictly followed monastic rules. He, too, went to China for a year of study. He returned with many different Buddhist teachings which he combined with one another and with *kami* worship. He called his teaching Tendai Buddhism. Mount Hiei became the major monastic center in Japan until its destruction in the sixteenth century. Its success, though, eventually undid Saicho's vision because its wealth bred disagreement and corruption. The monastery also excluded women. At first women had been denied access to the monastery to prevent sexual misconduct on the part of the monks, but eventually women themselves were seen as inferior and a source of defilement. Fortunately, later reformers, especially in the Pure Land school, asserted that women were spiritually equal to men.

Among the teachings Saicho brought back from China was Pure Land Buddhism. In Saicho's school of Tendai Buddhism, the recitation of the name Amitabha (*Amida* in Japanese) was practiced during rituals for the dead and as a means of gaining merit for the attainment of enlightenment. In the tenth century, however, a series of earthquakes and floods hit Kyoto, Japan's capital. The belief arose that it was already the age of Degenerated Dharma, an era in which a simple practice would be most effective for all people. This led several Tendai monks to emphasize the recitation of Amida's name, and they went out among the general population to preach. They were so successful that by the twelfth century, Pure Land Buddhism had become a separate sect.

The following tenth-century story describes how to worship Amida in order to be reborn in his Pure Land:

> **Now this Buddha [Amida] made a great vow for the sake of all sentient beings on this earth. The sentient beings of this earth have a great affinity with this Buddha. At the sound of one utterance of his name, sins from eighty billion kalpas [eons] of former life will be erased, and you will be reborn in that land where your outstretched arms can reach beyond the boundaries of a million billion lands. Those who want to reach the Pure Land must despise this**

world and pray for that one. Whether you are standing or sitting, despise your body for all its sufferings. Whether you are asleep or awake, pray for the joys of that other world. In the morning, when you see the lovely flowers of spring, you should yearn for the beauty of the Grove of Seven Rows [in the Pure Land], and in the evening when you hear the autumn winds, you should imagine the sound of the rippling Waters of the Eight Good Qualities. At the end of each day let your heart follow the setting sun into the west. There is no doubt about the good effect of good intentions acted upon for one day or one instant. Trust in this . . . and you will surely be reborn there.

The simplicity of this worship made it accessible to everyone, from the poorest farmer to the richest aristocrat. The great compassion of Amida is said to extend to all beings. In this way, the Pure Land sect avoided the exclusiveness of Tendai and Shingon Buddhism and also actively included women.

Political events also aided the spread of the Pure Land sect and other forms of Buddhism among the general population. At the end of the twelfth century, the warrior class, the samurai, gained political and military control of Japan. The activities of the royal court were reduced to ritual functions that had no effective power. This also meant the end of imperial control of Buddhism, which was now free to develop on its own. Monks established sects that permitted them to marry, and in the thirteenth century the monk Nichiren (1222–1282) established the *Lotus Sutra* as the main Buddhist text. Nichiren also recommended the practice of repeating the mantra *nam myoho renge kyo*, which means "homage to the *Lotus Sutra*," as a means of salvation.

Nichiren, who lived through a period of political upheaval, foreign invasions, and natural disasters, believed it was the age of Degenerated Dharma and that only this simple practice could save people. He was critical of other Buddhist practices and believed himself to be the buddha of the age of Degenerated Dharma.

Ch'an Buddhism, called Zen in Japanese, became prominent due to the work of two teachers: Eisai (1141–1215) and Dogen (1200–1253), monks who had studied in China. Dogen introduced the Sōtō school of Zen, which minimizes the use of koans and emphasizes meditation. The form of Zen proposed by Eisai, known as Rinzai, became popular among the samurai class, which admired its one-on-one confrontational style. Rinzai Zen was gradually incorporated into *bushido*, the code of the warrior, and was used to justify Japan's aggressive military policy in the nineteenth and twentieth centuries.

An example of the blending of Buddhism and the warrior code can be seen in a letter the Zen master Takuan (1573–1645) wrote to the greatest fencing master of his day:

> **Where should a swordsman fix his mind? If he puts his mind on the physical movement of his opponent, it will be seized by the movement; if he places it on the sword of his opponent, it will be arrested by the sword; if he focuses his mind on the thought of striking his opponent, it will be carried away by the very thought; if the mind stays on his own sword, it will be captured by his sword; if he centers it on the**

thought of not being killed by his opponent, his mind will be overtaken by this very thought; if he keeps his mind firmly on his own or on his opponent's posture, likewise, it will be blocked by them. Thus the mind should not be fixed anywhere.

• • •

Set your mind free as you would set the cat free; then your mind will work freely, unfixed, wherever it may go. Apply this to the mastery of swordsmanship: Do not let your mind stop, trying to figure out how to strike; forget how; strike without fixing your mind on the opponent.

From the standpoint of Zen Buddhism, to be self-conscious is not only to fail as a swordsman but also to be in a deluded state. Zen meditation leads to an awakened state that pervades all thought and activity even when the person is not meditating. The person simply is, without attachment to any outer being or object and without the distraction of any inner emotions such as fear or the desire to win.

Women, too, participated in the fierce side of Zen. Ryonen Genso (1646–1711) demonstrated the steely determination it requires as well as the sensitivity of its artistry. She was a beautiful and highly educated court lady who wanted to become a Zen nun, but the abbot of the monastery refused to admit her because he felt her beauty would distract the monks. Ryonen then took a hot iron brand and burned both sides of her face, leaving permanent scars. The following is her poem about this:

Formerly to amuse myself at court I would burn
orchid incense;
Now to enter the Zen life I burn my own face.
The four seasons pass by naturally like this.
But I don't know who I am amidst the change.
In this living world
the body I give up and burn
would be wretched
if I thought of myself as
anything but firewood.

Tibet

In the seventh century, the Yarlung dynasty solidified its rule in central Tibet, expanded its borders, and quickly became the dominant military power in central Asia—a position that it would hold for about two centuries. The second of the Yarlung kings, Songtsan Gampo, who died about 650, is traditionally regarded as Tibet's first Buddhist king. He is said to have been converted by two of his wives, one Nepali and the other Chinese. Both were Buddhists and are credited with bringing Buddhism to Tibet. At that time the people of Tibet followed a mixture of Chinese, Indian, and Iranian religious practices as well as native shamanism. Despite the influence of the king and his queens, many of the nobles and most of the Tibetan people preferred those practices over Buddhism.

A century later, even though Buddhism was still rejected by some nobles and of little interest to the larger population, King Trisong Detsan (742–797) made it the state religion. The first

Tibetan Buddhist monks were ordained and a great monastery built. Many Indian monks traveled to Tibet to help in the process of spreading Buddhism. By this time Tibet had conquered several of the Silk Road city-states. They were mostly Buddhist, and many of the occupying Tibetan soldiers and administrators were converted by the Buddhist cultures they encountered there.

The most important Buddhist missionary to Tibet in the eighth century was Padmasambhava, an Indian *siddha* and miracle worker, who embodied Vajrayana Buddhism. To this day he is worshipped as the second Buddha. Padmasambhava is especially honored for his ability to subdue the demonic forces that were believed to oppose the spread of Buddhism in Tibet, which he did through his mastery of tantric rituals. It is said that when a huge demoness opposed the building of the first monastery, Padmasambhava used his tantric powers to subdue her, and over her prone body he had the monastery built. He then traveled throughout Tibet performing miracles and subduing all other demons or deities that opposed Buddhism.

Royal support for Buddhism came to an end in the ninth century when an anti-Buddhist king, Lang Darma, began persecuting Buddhists. His assassination contributed to the downfall of the monarchy and introduced a period of political and religious chaos that lasted for almost two centuries. There was no centralized Tibetan government until the seventeenth century. Unlike other parts of Asia, Tibetan Buddhism developed without governmental controls or support.

There were three main types of religious experts in Tibetan Buddhism: scholar-monks in large monastery estates, monks and nuns in small village monasteries, and wonder-working yogis who wandered freely without fixed homes. All three followed Tantric practices and rituals. Some monks married, as did some yogis. Though there were many Tibetan nuns, they did not receive full ordinations—this ceremony may never have entered Tibet—nor did they receive the best educations or the highest initiations. Village nuns and monks performed ceremonies for the villagers, such as those for protecting the crops. The scholar-monks of Tibet performed the massive task of translating numerous Sanskrit texts into Tibetan. Today many of the Sanskrit originals have been lost and exist only in the Tibetan translations. In the thirteenth century, scholar-monks began to standardize the texts they had received from India and created the Tibetan Buddhist Canon. Like the Pali Canon, it contains rules for nuns and monks and many Mahayana and Vajrayana Buddhist works.

A leading example of the wandering yogi is Tibet's most beloved saint, Milarepa (1040–1123), who is known for the beauty of his poems and the strictness of his practice. When he was still a boy, his father died and relatives cheated him out of his inheritance. His mother then sent him to study black magic so that she and he could avenge themselves. He later committed several harmful acts against his relatives. Because of the negative karma that Milarepa acquired from his youthful bad deeds, his guru—Marpa (1012–1096)—put him through many ordeals to test his resolve before initiating him into tantric practices.

Tantric Buddhism is called Vajrayana in Tibet and the countries of the Himalayan Mountains, such as Nepal and Bhutan. It emphasizes the importance of the guru, an experienced teacher who can perform initiations and who possesses wisdom and full knowledge of Vajrayana Buddhism's intricate rituals. Indeed the guru is often added to the first three refuges: the Buddha, the Dharma, and the *Sangha*. Gurus typically demanded total obedience and dedication from their disciples. Milarepa had to trust the wisdom of his guru when Marpa had him build one huge tower after another, only to order them torn down as soon as they were finished. Milarepa's biography is an example of both the fierce quality of the guru-disciple relationship and the great compassion that underlies it.

For centuries, religious individuals of all three types (scholar-monks, village monks, and yogis) made the arduous journey from Tibet, over the mountains across Nepal, and into India to study directly with Buddhist masters and to receive initiations. Those who survived the journey returned to Tibet and attracted disciples. Among these seekers was Milarepa's guru, Marpa, who made several journeys to India to collect oral and written teachings to bring to Tibet. Life in India, however, was soon to change.

Beginning in the eleventh century, Muslim warriors slowly but steadily migrated into western India and gradually spread across

Treatment of the Dead

One goal of tantric practice is to overcome the fear of death, which causes followers to perform rituals and meditate in cemeteries. Pre-Buddhist beliefs in Tibet included rituals to make sure that the dead did not disturb the living. The combination of tantric and pre-Buddhist rituals led to the development of *Bardo* practice. The *Bardo* is the intermediary state between death and rebirth, in which the spirit roams for forty-nine days. Experts in Tantric Buddhism are believed to be able to liberate from the wheel of rebirth while in the *Bardo*, but less adept Tibetan Buddhists believe they will be disoriented, afraid, and confused and that they will reincarnate in the womb of their next mother. Specially trained monks conduct a ceremony for the forty-nine-day period during which they act as guides for the dead, attempting to lead them to liberation or, failing that, to a good rebirth.

northern and central India. In response to this, many Buddhist teachers fled north into the Himalayan Mountains, enriching the religious life of Tibet and Nepal. As the Buddhist monasteries and universities of India and their great libraries were destroyed, Tibet became a center of Buddhist learning.

Many large and powerful monasteries developed throughout Tibet. They owned vast estates that housed thousands of monks. In addition to monks who were scholars, many had other talents necessary for the operation of the large monasteries. Some monks were painters or makers of ritual objects; others supervised the monasteries' farms and grazing lands. They were also doctors and teachers. Often the monasteries were the only authority in their region so the head of the monastery also served as a secular (non-religious) ruler. Having monks who were the monastic and secular leaders led to the institution of the Dalai Lamas, the religious and political rulers of Tibet. Dalai Lamas are believed to be incarnations of the celestial bodhisattva Avalokitesvara, the protector of Tibet, and exemplify the concept of the *dharmaraja*, the king who merges worldly and spiritual power. The first Dalai Lama to successfully establish this position was the fifth, Nawang Lozang Gyatso (1617–1682). His predecessors had converted the Mongols, the most powerful military force in Asia at that time, to the Buddhist faith. With the Mongols' help, the Fifth Dalai Lama was able, for the most part, to centralize Tibet's government in Lhasa and to become one of the most revered living beings for most Tibetans.

Central to the Dalai Lama system is the belief that the Dalai Lama is an incarnation of Avalokitesvara and that shortly after a Dalai Lama dies, Avalokitesvara reincarnates again as the next Dalai Lama. Two or three years after the death of a Dalai Lama, senior monks watch for miraculous signs and omens that will lead them to find the new Dalai Lama. Once the Dalai Lama is found—he could be born almost anywhere—the monks install him in the Tibetan capital, Lhasa. While the young Dalai Lama grows up, another monk rules in his place.

Going on pilgrimage was, and remains, a popular practice among laypeople and monastics, even though travel through Tibet was difficult and sometimes even dangerous during unsettled times. The capital city, Lhasa, home of the Dalai Lamas, was a favorite destination. Some pilgrims hoped to increase the merit they would receive from making such a pilgrimage by performing full-body-length prostrations all the way to Lhasa. Other pilgrims instead circumambulated the city doing prostrations. Pilgrims often wore pads on their hands and knees to help them physically endure this practice. Once in Lhasa, pilgrims would worship at its famous shrines, temples, and monasteries, such as the Jokhang Temple, said to have been built by King Songstan Gampo in the seventh century. Many pilgrims, as they

A Tibetan woman spins her prayer wheel as she makes her way along the street.

walked along the roads or ritually circled the shrines, carried a prayer wheel in their right hands.

Generally, prayer wheels are cylindrical metal cases about 3 to 4 inches (7.6 to 10 centimeters) high and about twice that length around, mounted on a wooden or metal handle so that it can be turned with the aid of a small weight attached to the outside of the case by a chain. The cases contain mantras written countless times on a long, narrow, tightly wound-up piece of paper. The mantra is usually that of Avalokitesvara, *om mani padme hum*. Tibetans believe that with each turn of the prayer wheels, the mantras are activated just as if they were said aloud. There are also much larger prayer wheels in monasteries and around other sacred places. Similarly, Tibetans hang prayer flags—brightly colored cloths with prayers written on them—from the roofs of their houses, in trees, and over streams, trusting that the wind will carry their prayers.

Pilgrimages to the many sacred mountains of Tibet were also

Colorful prayer flags flit in the breeze in Lhasa, Tibet. Buddhists believe the wind carries and disperses the prayers printed on the flags.

popular, and these often involved rituals to pacify local spirits and the Buddhist deities associated with the mountains. The Himalayas are the highest mountains in the world, having steep narrow paths that make them very dangerous. Yet the pilgrims circumambulated the mountain, some even covering the distance by performing full prostrations rather than by walking.

four

MODERN BUDDHISM IN ASIA

Modern Buddhism in Asia began around the sixteenth century with the arrival of European traders, many of whom grew rich from the lucrative spice trade. More merchants followed and eventually various European countries established colonies, which led to the rise of nationalism. In Sri Lanka and Southeast Asia, colonial rule meant taking away the power of native kings, who had been the main financial supporters of Buddhism. Western colonization also supplied a supportive environment for Christian missionaries, many of whom were hostile to other faiths. They often attacked Buddhism as being merely a superstition practiced by ignorant people.

Ceylon, now known as Sri Lanka, is an example of Western intolerance. It was colonized in the early sixteenth century by the Portuguese, who destroyed monasteries, persecuted Buddhists, and forcibly converted them to Catholicism. When, in turn, the Dutch and British took control, they urged Catholics and Buddhists alike to become Protestants. Although less repressive than the Portuguese, the Dutch and the British mounted active campaigns to discredit Buddhism. In the 1860s, however, a young Buddhist novice turned the tables on the British colonizers. His name was Mohottiwatte Gunananda. He had received a Christian education, which he put to good use against Christian missionaries by holding a series of public debates with them. In 1873 he won a week-long public debate that not only earned him the support of his fellow Celanese, he caught the attention and gained the backing of Westerners.

In the late nineteenth century, many Westerners were attracted to the religions of Asia. Among them were Helena Petrovna Blavatsky and Henry Steel Olcott, founders of the Theosophical Society, which was an extremely popular movement among some of the most influential people of the nineteenth century. In 1889 they traveled to Ceylon and publicly took refuge in the Three Jewels; in other words, they publicly converted to Buddhism. Blavatsky and Olcott not only converted to Buddhism, they campaigned to reform Buddhism. The people of Ceylon, both lay and monastic, joined forces with the foreigners, and a familiar pattern in Sri Lankan religious history was repeated—the purification of Buddhism. Blavatsky and Olcott examined the texts preserved in the Pali Canon to discover the practices and beliefs of early Buddhism. They compared the practices of the nineteenth century to those in the Pali Canon and denied the validity of any practice not found there. At the same time, Buddhism became a rallying point for the rebellious nationalist cause. By the time Sri Lanka won independence from England in 1948, Buddhist monks were politicized beings, and they remain active in politics today. The first Sri Lankan prime minister, S. W. R. D. Bandaranaike, promoted a form of Buddhist socialism. But not all Sri Lankans were Buddhists, and his policies—especially the promotion of Buddhism as the source of national identity—contributed to the civil war that has raged for more than twenty years between Hindus and Buddhists.

In Myanmar, formerly known as Burma during the period of British colonial rule (1886–1948), Buddhist monks were able to maintain their strong pattern of monastic scholarship. Like many other Southeast Asian Buddhists, Burmese Buddhists allow for temporary and short-term ordinations. When the British banned political gatherings in

Burma during the struggle for independence, many nationalists took up temporary ordination and used religious meetings at monasteries to preach political ideas to the laity.

In 1948 U Nu became the first prime minister of independent Burma, and, like his later counterpart in Sri Lanka, he sought to establish a government that blended socialism with Buddhism. Also like Sri Lanka, Burma contains many non-Buddhists and people of different backgrounds. He was overthrown by a military junta in 1962 that had a less religious agenda for the nation. Eventually, the new government started supporting monastic Buddhism as a way to rebuild its own crumbling popularity, while it also enforced state control over Buddhist monks.

Communist takeovers of the governments of Cambodia and Laos in 1975 were disastrous for Buddhism, especially in Cambodia where tens of thousands of monks were executed and innumerable monasteries destroyed. Today Buddhism is slowly recovering in these countries.

Thailand is the only nation in Southeast Asia that has never been colonized, though it was under constant threat from both the British and the French. Rama IV, who ruled from 1851 to 1868, was a strong king with excellent diplomatic skills, who managed to keep Westerners away. At the same time, he set in motion extensive reforms within the monastic community by requiring strict monastic discipline. He himself had been an ordained monk for thirty years before he ascended the throne and was quite familiar with monastic practices. His successor, Rama V, who ruled from 1868 to 1910, carried the changes even further by creating a national organization for Thai monks, starting ecclesiastical examinations on a national level, and controlling the ordination of monks. He wanted to standardize the knowledge of dharma throughout the country and to control advancement through the monastic hierarchy. To achieve these ends, he went so far as to destroy ancient texts that did not conform to the Pali Canon.

Since the colonial period, the major change in the Buddhism of Sri Lanka and Southeast Asia has been the deeper involvement of the laity. Before then, Buddhist laypeople were focused on achieving merit and leading moral lives. Gradually, the laity became more involved in the practice of meditation, and retreat centers were established for them. Today, Asian Buddhists are deeply involved with social and political issues along with meditation practices and the search for enlightenment. Colonialism, struggles for independence, the devastation of twentieth-century wars, and the problems of westernization and poverty have all caused a reinterpretation of dharma that confronts the suffering of the modern world. In recent years two Buddhist leaders have received the Nobel Peace Prize: the Fourteenth Dalai Lama in 1989 for his peaceful attempts to gain Tibetan independence from China, and Aung San Suu Kyi in 1991 for opposing the military regime of Myanmar. Monks and nuns were involved in opposing the Vietnam War; and in Thailand, Myanmar, Sri Lanka, and Vietnam they are actively participating in social welfare and education programs. In addition, throughout south and Southeast Asia, nuns are striving to raise their status as monastics.

The term *engaged Buddhism* was coined by the Vietnamese Ch'an monk Thich Nhat Hanh, born in 1926, to refer to Buddhist practice that is socially and politically involved. Buddhism in Vietnam had suffered under French colonization (1858–1954), which supported Roman Catholic missionary activity. The missionaries were particularly successful in South Vietnam. As in other parts of colonized Asia, upper-class Christian converts often became part of an important and powerful westernized elite. During the Vietnam War, the U.S. government supported that ruling elite in South Vietnam. The Communist regime in the north alternated between using and undermining Buddhism. Buddhist monks and nuns felt displaced by both regimes, and they actively opposed the war. Their most dramatic form of protest was setting themselves on fire. A monk or nun would douse him- or herself with gasoline and then strike a match. The world looked on, horrified.

In the mid-1960s, Thich Nhat Hanh wrote a letter to the American civil-rights activist Martin Luther King Jr., in which he explained that the monastics who set fire to themselves were not committing suicide. Rather, by enduring such a painful death, they were drawing attention to the importance of ending the war. For Thich Nhat Hanh, it recalled the story about a former life of Gautama Buddha, when he jumped off a cliff to give his body to a hungry tigress. For Thich Nhat Hanh, such self-sacrifice is the highest form of compassion and is central to the teachings of the Buddha. These sacrificing monastics also recall Miao-shan, when she sacrificed her eyes and arms for the benefit of her father. Such demonstrations of compassion are an ancient theme that is deeply present in Buddhist thought and practice.

Another example of socially and politically engaged Buddhism began in India, where Buddhism had all but disappeared due to the destruction of the monasteries by Muslim invaders and the absorption of many of its teachings into Hinduism. After India won independence from Great Britain in 1947, however, the political leader Dr. Bhimrao Ramji Ambedkar (1891–1956) led a mass conversion of Hindu untouchables, people at the lowest end of Indian society, to Buddhism. India has an ancient social system that connects status and ritual purity to the caste or group one is born into. Untouchables were those people placed so low in the social system that contact with them was considered polluting. Today they are referred to as among the scheduled castes, meaning that they are supposed to have reserved for them a certain number of places in schools and government jobs. Though Ambedkar himself was born into an untouchable family, he became a respected lawyer and drafted the Indian constitution. His father was an officer in the British army. Young Ambedkar went to school in India and then in the United States and England. Despite his accomplishments, when he returned to India he continually suffered from caste violence and discrimination. During the Indian independence movement, he attacked caste as the main issue although Mahatma Gandhi and Jawaharlal Nehru focused on the British.

The caste system is part of Hindu religious beliefs. Ambedkar said that the untouchables should choose their religion, not just accept Hinduism. He understood the importance of religion in the lives of Indians, and he wanted to remain within the Indian religious traditions rather than take on a foreign faith such as Christianity. He chose Buddhism, an Indian religion that traditionally had opposed the caste system. However, Ambedkar reinterpreted Buddhism. For instance, he rejected the Four Noble Truths, arguing that the teachings of the Buddha were not accurately transmitted due to their vastness and the limitations of oral transmission. The problem facing Ambedkar was that he knew traditional forms of Buddhism would not appeal to his followers and would not advance their social cause. He thought that karma and rebirth intensified self-blame for one's present situation and that the traditional form of monasticism, with its vows of poverty, was meaningless to a totally impoverished section of society. He emphasized the Buddha's concern with human suffering and located the source of that suffering outside the human being, in the injustice of a discriminatory social system and grinding poverty. He also advocated Buddhist virtues, such as compassion for others and the development of balance and wisdom, as able to uplift the oppressed and aid them in changing their situation. Ambedkar advocated social transformation through Buddhist principles.

Throughout its long history, Buddhism has been reinterpreted by great thinkers especially in new social settings, or at least different aspects of the Buddha's teachings have been emphasized over others. One need only recall the innovative teachings of Mahayana and

Vajrayana Buddhism. Interestingly, in the twentieth century Buddhism was almost extinct in its Indian homeland. Today Ambedkar's Buddhist community is flourishing, as is that of the Tibetan refugee community.

During the twentieth century, China underwent periods of violent upheaval, social chaos, and extreme political changes. The last royal dynasty, the Manchu, was overthrown in 1911, to be replaced by the Nationalist government, which allowed Buddhists a greater freedom than they had had in the past. This period came to an end with the rise of the Communist regime in 1949, which confiscated Buddhist properties and forced many nuns and monks to return to lay life. The situation worsened during the Cultural Revolution (1966–1976) when rampaging Red Guards, often just gangs of teenaged girls and boys, targeted Buddhist sites for destruction to speed the arrival of a reorganized society named "the new order."

Communism has proved hostile to religion wherever it has gained power. Buddhist institutions in China, Tibet, Mongolia, Cambodia, Laos, and other parts of Asia have suffered random and widespread destruction. Tens of thousands of Buddhist monastics have been brutally killed and others enslaved in forced-labor camps. Many Buddhist leaders now see communism as a movement they must fight if Buddhism is to survive.

The defeated Chinese Nationalist government fled to the island of Taiwan after the Communist takeover of mainland China in 1949, and there Buddhism has slowly begun a revival. Today, Taiwanese Buddhism is unusual in its large proportion of nuns and its large numbers of laywomen who support and participate in Buddhist practice. One of its most important institutions—the Tzu Chi Foundation—was started by a nun, Dharma Master Cheng Yen. It takes Kuan Yin as its model; that is, its followers try to act as Kuan Yin would by providing medical care as well as food and housing to the poor. The foundation also offers disaster relief throughout the world, including the United States, where it aids the inner-city poor and provides companionship for neglected patients in old-age homes.

Beginning in the seventeenth century, the Fifth Dalai Lama ruled over Tibet with the support of the Mongols. Later, other Dalai Lamas maintained their rule with the help of the Chinese. This history supports China's present claim to control of Tibet. Tibetan history is tumultuous and involves complex relationships with the Chinese imperial government. When the imperial government was overthrown in 1911, Tibet had involved dealings with the Nationalist government and then with the newly established Communist regime. Soon after the victory of the Communists in 1949, the Chinese Communist government announced that it would unite all of China, which from its perspective included Tibet. In 1950 the Chinese army marched into eastern Tibet and then started its march to the capital, Lhasa. The Fourteenth Dalai Lama, Tenzin Gyatso, was fifteen years old at the time. In the face of that crisis, he assumed full political and religious control of Tibet. The Tibetan government appealed to the United Nations for help, but could not be aided because Tibet was not a member of the United Nations. The undermanned and poorly equipped Tibetan army was no match for the Chinese army. On September 9, 1951, Chinese troops entered Lhasa and took control. The Communist government quickly began to institute profound changes in Chinese and in Tibetan society. Land was seized and redistributed, and people were organized into collectives that would, at least theoretically, equally share the work and its produce. Needless to say, not everyone wanted to live that way, especially the independently minded Tibetans.

Tensions between the Chinese officials in Lhasa and the young Dalai Lama continued to increase. In 1959 he fled to exile in India, where he continues to live. The Chinese declared martial law and began destroying and looting Tibet, especially its monasteries. The worst destruction occurred during China's Cultural Revolution, beginning in 1966, when China targeted Tibetan monasteries. Many monks and nuns actively opposed the Chinese occupation of their country and participated in the unsuccessful Tibetan uprising of 1987. Countless monks and nuns were imprisoned and were tortured and humiliated for years afterward.

In Tibet today, many of the monasteries have been rebuilt, though some of them are more like tourist shops than monasteries. The Chinese authorities carefully monitor the monasteries and nunneries, which they continue to view with suspicion since nuns and monks are still active in seeking Tibetan independence. In India there are approximately 100,000 Tibetan refugees who have rebuilt their monastic institutions and have established a government-in-exile under the Dalai Lama.

Numerous Westerners have been drawn to the plight of the Tibetan people and to the teachings of Tibetan Buddhism, especially those of the Dalai Lama. In responding to the Chinese occupation of Tibet, the Dalai Lama has developed a philosophy of social transformation based on Buddhism. He argues that most of the serious problems facing humanity today are caused by human beings, therefore the only way to change this situation is to change human beings one by one. His point is that to make the world a better place, each person has to undergo a personal spiritual transformation. In other words, achieving world peace begins with achieving inner peace. One can work on oneself, while working for the good of others, however, but the need for personal transformation will always be central. He recommends that people recognize the interdependence of all the world's people and the equality of everyone—ideas connected to Buddhist beliefs that everyone possesses buddha nature. He also advocates the Buddhist virtue of compassion, which he interprets to mean loving all other people, even enemies. The notion of Buddhist compassion is illustrated by the bodhisattva who puts all live beings before her or himself. The

A Tibetan man holds his grandson, believed by some to be a reincarnated lama. The child holds a prayer wheel. Despite the challenges presented Tibet in the form of Chinese occupation, Buddhism still thrives in the mountainous region.

Dalai Lama says:

> **Although to bring about inner change is difficult, it is absolutely worthwhile to try. This is my firm belief. What is important is that we try our best. Whether we succeed or not is a different question. Even if we could not achieve what we seek within this life, it is all right; at least we will have made the attempt to form a better human society on the basis of love—true love—and less selfishness.**

In one sense, the Dalai Lama has moved beyond just seeking independence for Tibet, to trying to influence how the entire world cares for itself and for all the people in it.

Japan resisted colonization during the Tokugawa era (1603–1868) and restricted the activities of Christian missionaries. However, the Tokugawa government favored Confucianism and the Shinto faith as unifying forces in Japanese society and withdrew all funding from Buddhist institutions. Despite this, individual Buddhist teachers continued to attract followers and to compose outstanding texts and works of art.

In 1868 the Japanese emperor was restored to power, and this government was initially quite hostile to Buddhism. The government seized a great deal of Buddhist property and changed the face of Japanese Buddhism in two important ways. First, it issued a decree that Buddhist monks should be allowed to marry, with the result that today there are few celibate monks in Japan, although nuns have maintained their vows of celibacy.

The second change developed in relation to the government's aggressive militaristic policy. A new generation of Buddhist scholars redefined Buddhism in relation to Japanese nationalism and Western rationalism and science. The Rinzai branch of Zen was the most successful at this. Its priests insisted on Zen's connection to the warrior's code of manly self-sacrifice, discipline, and fearlessness. This view opposed Western criticisms that Asian men were effeminate, at the same time that it supported the national war effort and expansionist policy that began with the Sino-Japanese War (1894–1895) and did not end until Japan's defeat in World War II.

After World War II, Japanese society maintained Confucian and Buddhist values, which were redirected toward economic success. New religions also flourished, many of which claimed connections with Buddhism. One of the most successful, both in Japan and abroad, is Soka Gakkai. It follows the monk Nichiren's practice of chanting the name of the *Lotus Sutra* but has expanded the belief that spiritual benefits and material benefits are related to one another, so chanting for worldly benefits like good grades, financial success, and the lessening of physical and mental problems is acceptable.

Korean Buddhism experienced persecution during the Yi Dynasty (1392–1910), but its practice continued among the general population. The rising influence of Christianity in the nineteenth century led to a small Buddhist revival. In the early twentieth century, the practice of Ch'an or Son Buddhism spread, especially through the efforts of Mang Gong (1872–1946) who taught not only monks, but also nuns and laypeople. These developments were sidetracked when Japan took over Korea in 1910 as part of its program of military aggression. The Japanese supported Buddhism in Korea as they did in Japan, but they wanted to control Korean Buddhism and have their form of Zen be dominant. They also wanted Buddhist monks to renounce their vows of celibacy and to marry. This led some Korean monks to oppose the Japanese, but many also married. The legacy of this conflict is a divided Buddhist monastic community in Korea. After the Japanese left in 1945, those monks who remained celibate demanded that the monks who had married be thrown out of their monasteries and out of the order. The married priests then formed their own order.

This hand-colored albumen print shows two Japanese monks of the 1870s, the start of a period of radical transformation for Buddhism in Japan.

These South Korean nuns pray during festivities honoring the Buddha's birthday.

Today in South Korea the orders of monks and nuns are very strong. Although few monks or nuns practice the intense meditation of the Ch'an tradition, for the most part they keep to their vows, some choosing a life of social service within their rapidly changing society. In North Korea, however, it is assumed that Buddhists are not allowed to practice their religion.

Throughout Asia today there is great acceptance of Western converts to Buddhism. Asian Buddhists at pilgrimage sites welcome Western practitioners and readily explain the proper way to participate. Many renowned Asian Buddhist gurus accept Western disciples. For approximately 2,500 years, Buddhism has been a religion that welcomes and seeks out converts of any race and faith. Its enduring success can be seen in the West today.

five

BUDDHISM IN THE UNITED STATES

Buddhism in the United States began with the immigration of East Asians, such as the Chinese who first came to California in 1849 at the start of the gold rush. They brought their faith with them. Their Buddhism was a mix of Mahayana Buddhism and the native Chinese religions of Taoism and Confucianism. In contrast, the Japanese first immigrated in 1868 to Hawaii, where they worked on plantations. Japanese missionaries founded the Buddhist Church of America in 1899, which follows the format of Christian churches, for example by having Sunday morning worship services. Additionally, Buddhism caught the interest of American intellectuals and philosophers, who believed non-European cultures had something to offer the West. From its beginnings in America, Buddhism has been divided along racial lines: temples and centers created by and for Asian immigrants and their descendants, and centers created by and for Western converts. Five or six million Buddhists live in America, 80 percent of whom are of Asian descent.

In 1893 the World Parliament of Religions, a meeting of representatives from almost all of the world's great religions, was held in Chicago. This meeting was extensively covered by the press and it introduced many forms of world religion to Americans of European descent, or Euro-Americans. A young Theravada Buddhist monk from Sri Lanka, Anagarika Dharmapala (1864–1933), especially caught the attention of the American public. Dharmapala had close

A young Western convert to Buddhism.

ties to the Theosophical Society, though he later broke with it, and he became a leading force in reclaiming the main Buddhist pilgrimage sites in India, especially Bodh Gaya, which at that time was being run by a Hindu priest. He also converted the first Euro-American to Buddhism. Dharmapala devoted the remainder of his life to lecturing in the United States and the rest of the world, gaining many Euro-American converts, and contributing to the revival of Buddhism in Asia—especially in Sri Lanka.

The Rinzai branch of Zen Buddhism also made an impression on the American public during the World Parliament of Religions. Its representative, Shaku Soen, was invited in 1905 to return to the United States to teach Zen. His teaching led to the establishment of Zen centers that continue today on the West Coast and in New York City. The greatest influence, though, came from his disciple D. T. Suzuki (1870–1966), the primary interpreter of Zen in the West. In his writings and personal appearances, Suzuki argued that Zen was not limited to a Buddhist context, but that it could be practiced by anyone of any faith. This had great appeal to many Euro-Americans. Other Zen teachers, however, established meditation centers in the United States, where Westerners could follow strict Zen practices within a context of Buddhist values and morality.

In the United States, Tibetan Vajrayana Buddhism is dominated by Euro-Americans, although Tibetan monastics play important parts as teachers. Few American converts know any lay Tibetans; they know only monks and teachers. In part this is due to the very small number of Tibetan refugees that have been allowed into the United States and the fact that, although most Tibetan Buddhists practice in monasteries, Tibetans living in the West do not necessarily practice in monasteries. Rather they practice at home through the maintenance of a shrine or through private chanting and prayer. Most do not do so. In Tibet, laypeople rarely performed the more intensive tantric practices; but in the United States, Euro-American laypeople are eager to participate in them.

Today Buddhism, in its many varieties, is an established religion in the United States with strong monasteries and retreat centers. Yet, for the most part, a breach remains between the Buddhism brought over by Asian immigrants and that of Western practitioners. On the one hand, for people of Asian descent, Buddhism is part of their cultural heritage and they have little interest in reaching out to the larger Euro-American community. On the other hand, numerous Western Buddhists have taken Buddhist ideas out of context. For instance, some practice Buddhist meditation but ignore its moral and ethical teachings or divorce Buddhism from its cultural heritage and interpret the tradition freely. So, many Asian Americans feel Euro-Americans neither respect nor understand Buddhism, while some Euro-Americans feel Asian Americans confuse Buddhism with Asian culture. Both groups also read Buddhist history differently. Buddhism has proved itself to be very adaptable to new environments. For Westerners this means that Buddhism will once again adapt to its new home in America. Asian Americans focus on another side of Buddhist history, the continual tendency to reform, to return to its roots, either by the kings who purified the monastic orders, or the Chinese pilgrim-monks who made the difficult and dangerous journey to India to get the purest teachings of the Buddha, or the contemporary Asian movements for a more socially meaningful Buddhism. Consequently, Asian Americans feel that Buddhism must make an effort to remain true to its Asian roots in the United States as it has elsewhere in Asia.

An exception to the breach between Asian American and Euro-American Buddhist practitioners can be seen in the work of Thich Nhat Hanh. To protest the Vietnam War in 1966, he made a trip to the United States to appeal for peace. At the end of this trip, neither of the warring regimes in Vietnam would allow him to return to his native

A bust of Buddha and a prayer necklace are gathered in a bowl. Some Americans have co-opted or borrowed the trappings and iconography of Buddhism without fully learning its precepts or integrating them into their lives.

land. He continued his work, living in exile and traveling the world, lecturing and writing books on the theme of engaged Buddhism, a practice that blends meditation and social service. He has a large following among Westerners, many of whom live in the United States, but he also has a large following among Vietnamese refugees. As part of his practice of engaged Buddhism, he holds meditation retreats during which Vietnamese refugees and American Vietnam War veterans meet so that both sides can heal from the damage of that war.

Another exception are two sects of Nichiren Buddhism, Soka Gakkai and Nichiren Shoshu, both of which have Asian and non-Asian members. In fact, Soka Gakkai is the only Buddhist group in America with a sizable number of African American and Hispanic members. As in the past, the simplicity of its practice, chanting the name of the *Lotus Sutra*, makes it accessible to people from all walks of life.

Many Buddhist publishers are flourishing in the United States, and there is an enormous amount of information available on the Internet, all of which is having an impact on American Buddhism. Such availability was not possible until fairly recently and marks a real break with Buddhist practice. One has to wonder what will happen to American Buddhism if students no longer enter into highly personal, charged relationships with their teachers but instead participate only electronically or by reading books.

TIME LINE

SOUTH ASIA

566–486 B.C.E.
Lifetime of the Buddha

about 270–230 B.C.E.
Emperor Asoka's reign. Buddhism becomes the state religion of India.

SOUTHEAST ASIA

about 250 B.C.E.
Emperor Asoka sends Buddhist missionaries to Sri Lanka. It becomes the state religion of Sri Lanka.

third century B.C.E.
Indian and Sri Lankan merchants and monks take Buddhism to Burma.

first century B.C.E.
Pali Canon written in Sri Lanka.

first century C.E.
Buddhist traders and monks take Buddhism to Cambodia.

third century
Buddhism reaches Vietnam from both India and China.

fifth century
Buddhism reaches Indonesia.

eleventh to thirteenth centuries
Theravada Buddhism sweeps through Cambodia, Thailand, and Laos.

eleventh century
King Anawrahta of Burma (ruled 1040–1077) of Burma promotes Theravada.

twelfth century
Burmese monks take Theravada to Cambodia, where it becomes the state religion.

thirteenth century
Thai state develops and adopts Theravada Buddhism from Burma. It becomes the state religion.

fourteenth century
Laos develops as a state. Theravada becomes the state religion.

sixteenth century onward
Decline of Buddhism under European colonial rule

nineteenth century onward
Decline of Buddhism under European colonial rule.

Buddhist revivals aided by Euro-American scholars and the theosophical movement. Buddhism takes root in the West.

South, Central, and East Asia

about 100–200 C.E.
Rise of Mahayana Buddhism in northern India.

about 100 C.E.
Buddhist missionaries enter China from India, central Asia, and Sri Lanka.

about fourth century
Buddhist missionaries enter Korea from India and China. Buddhism becomes the state religion in the seventh century.

about fifth century
Rise of Vajrayana Buddhism in northern India.

about 552
Introduction of Buddhism to Japan from Korea and China. Buddhism becomes the state religion in the seventh century.

about 700
Introduction of Buddhism to Tibet. It is made the state religion in the eighth century.

GLOSSARY

arhat—A nun or monk who has achieved enlightenment and therefore is believed not to reincarnate.

bodhisattva—An enlightened being who has vowed to become a buddha but who postpones final buddhahood to continue to reincarnate in order to help other beings achieve enlightenment; can be female, male, divine, human, animal, dead, or living.

buddha—One who has achieved enlightenment.

Ch'an—A Chinese form of Buddhism that follows the Mahayana school and emphasizes meditation practices; called Zen in Japan and Son in Korea.

compassion—The main quality of all buddhas and bodhisattvas, whether human or divine. It is an active virtue. Someone who is compassionate acts or speaks to lessen another's suffering. All Buddhists attempt to be compassionate to all living things.

Degenerated Dharma—The final period of Buddhist decline.

dharma—Buddhist doctrine, what the Buddha taught; also one's own duty.

enlightenment—An awakening to ultimate reality that frees one from desire and bestows supernatural powers such as unlimited wisdom.

guru—A spiritual teacher.

jataka—A story about a previous life of Gautama Buddha.

kami—Sacred beings, objects, and places that in Japan were believed to possess spiritual power.

karma—The result of one's good and bad deeds.

Mahayana—A school of Buddhism believed to contain the private doctrine of the Buddha. Ch'an and Pure Land are both forms of Mahayana. Vajrayana Buddhism incorporates Mahayana teachings.

mantra—Syllables and Sanskrit words that, when recited, grant power over certain deities or invoke celestial buddhas and bodhisattvas.

merit—The result of making offerings to nuns or monks, chanting, going on a pilgrimage, and practicing Buddhist virtues. It enriches one person's spiritual future or can be dedicated to someone else.

nirvana—Non-existence.

Pure Land—A heaven that is purified by the presence and teachings of a buddha. It is also a school of Buddhism.

relic—A part of the body or memento of a dead holy person.

samsara—The existing world.

sangha—The Buddhist community, meaning either monks and nuns or all Buddhists.

shamanism—A religion in which a spiritual leader takes trancelike ritual journeys to meet and subdue deities and demons in order to gain their powers.

siddha—A wandering yogi who also works wonders.

Son—Korean for *Ch'an*.

stupa—A solid architectural structure that houses the bodily relics of the Buddha or another important Buddhist figure.

Tantric Buddhism—The same as Vajrayana Buddhism.

Theravada—An early school of Buddhism.

Three Jewels—The Buddha, the Dharma, and the *Sangha*.

Vajrayana—A school of Buddhism that incorporates Mahayana teachings as well as many magical and shamanic elements.

Zen—Japanese for *Ch'an*.

FURTHER RESOURCES

BOOKS

BIOGRAPHIES OF THE BUDDHA:

Bays, Gwendolyn, trans. *The Voice of the Buddha: The Beauty of Compassion*. Oakland, CA: Dharma, 1983.

Cowell, E. B., ed. *The Jatakā*. London: Pali Text Society, 1973.

Davids, T. W. Rhys, trans. *The Mahāparinibbāna Suttanta* in *Buddhist Suttas*. Oxford, England: Oxford University Press, 1881.

Johnston, E. H., ed. and trans. *Buddhacarita*. Delhi, India: Motilal Barnarsidass, 1984.

SOME SOURCES ON THE EARLY PERIOD OF BUDDHISM:

Gombrich, Richard. *Theravada Buddhism: A Social History from Ancient Benares to Modern Colombo*. London and New York: Routledge and Kegan Paul, 1988.

Gomez, Luis O. "Buddhism: Buddhism in India." In the *Encyclopedia of Religion*, ed. by Mircea Eliade, vol. XX. New York: Macmillan Publishing Company, 1987.

MORE GENERAL STUDIES OF BUDDHISM ARE:

de Bary, William Theodore, ed. *The Buddhist Tradition in India, China and Japan.* New York: Vintage Books, 1972.

Conze, Edward, et al, trans. *Buddhist Texts through the Ages.* New York: Harper & Row, 1964.

Robinson, Richard H., Willard L. Johnson, et al. *The Buddhist Religion: A Historical Introduction*, 4th ed. Belmont, CA: Wadsworth Publishing, 1997.

Strong, John S. *The Experience of Buddhism: Sources and Interpretations.* Belmont, CA: Wadsworth Publishing, 1994.

Swearer, Donald K. *The Buddhist World of Southeast Asia.* Albany, NY: State University of New York Press, 1995.

SOURCES ON GENDER AND BUDDHISM:

Bartholomeusz, Tessa. *Women under the Bō Tree: Buddhist Nuns in Sri Lanka*. Cambridge, England: Cambridge University Press, 1994.

Cabezón, José Ignacio, ed. *Buddhism, Sexuality, and Gender.* Albany, NY: State University of New York Press, 1992.

Horner, I. B. *Women under Primitive Buddhism.* Delhi, India: Motilal Barnasidass, 1975.

Paul, Diana. *Women in Buddhism: Images of the Feminine in the Mahāyāna Tradition.* Berkeley: University of California Press, 1985.

Shaw, Miranda. *Passionate Enlightenment: Women in Tantric Buddhism.* Princeton, NJ: Princeton University Press, 1994.

Tsai, Katherine Ann, trans. *Lives of the Nuns: Biographies of Chinese Buddhist Nuns from the Fourth to Sixth Centuries.* Honolulu: University of Hawaii Press, 1994.

Tsomo, Karma Lekshe, ed. *Sakyadhītā: Daughters of the Buddha.* Ithaca, NY: Snow Lion Publications, 1988.

Young, Serinity. *Courtesans and Tantric Consorts: Sexualities in Buddhist Narrative, Iconography, and Ritual.* New York: Routledge, 2004.

CONTEMPORARY BUDDHISM:

Fields, Rick. *How the Swans Came to the Lake: A Narrative History of Buddhism in America.* 3rd ed. Boston: Shambhala Publications, 1992.

Presbish, Charles S., and Kenneth K. Tanaka. *The Faces of Buddhism in America*. Berkeley: University of California Press, 1998.

Queen, Christopher S., and Sallie B. King, eds. *Engaged Buddhism: Buddhist Liberation Movements in Asia*. Albany, NY: State University of New York Press, 1996.

WEB SITES

The following Web sites have an enormous number of links to other Buddhist sites:

http://www.dharmanet.org

http://www.buddhanet.net

Web sites for Buddhist films:

http://www.teach-buddhism.mcgill.ca

http://www.mysticfire.com

FILMOGRAPHY

Being the Buddha in L.A. Boston: WGBH, 1993. Color video. Cambodian Buddhism in Los Angeles.

Blue Collar and Buddha. Siegel Productions, 1987. Color video. Laotian Buddhists in Rockford, Illinois.

Buddhism, Footprint of the Buddha. Time-Life Video, 1977. Color film and video. Buddhism in Sri Lanka.

Kundun. Buena Vista Pictures, 1997. Color film and video. The life of Tenzin Gyatso, the present Dalai Lama of Tibet.

Little Buddha. Miramax Films, 1994. Color film and video. The life of the Buddha.

Vesak. New York: Focus International, Inc., 1975. Color film. The Sri Lankan festival of Vesak, a celebration of the birth, enlightenment, and death of the Buddha.

SOURCE NOTES

Chapter One:

p. 16: "I have freely made. . . ." Gwendolyn Bays, trans., *The Voice of the Buddha* (Oakland, CA: Dharma Press, 1983), p. 480.

p. 16: "revealed the upper half of her body" Bays, *Voice*, p. 482.

p. 18: "I was such and such a person. . . ." Bays, *Voice*, p. 518.

p. 19: "they [were] endowed with good conduct. . . ." Bays, *Voice*, p. 614.

p. 24: "One day, bathing my feet. . . ." Davids, trans. *Psalms of the Early Buddhists*, (London: Pali Text Society, 1980), part I, p. 73. Translation slightly modified.

p. 25: "There are four places. . . ." T. W. Rhys Davids, trans. *Buddhist Suttas* (Oxford, England: Oxford University Press, 1881), pp. 90–91.

Chapter Two:

p. 40: "I pay homage to the perfection of wisdom! . . ." Edward Conze, et al, trans. *Buddhist Texts through the Ages* (New York: Harper & Row, 1964), p. 146.

Chapter Three:

p. 54: "is a pleasant and prosperous kingdom. . . ." James Legge, trans., *A Record of Buddhistic Kingdoms* (New York: Dover Publications, 1965), p. 16. Translation slightly modified.

p. 55: "When (the cart) was a hundred paces. . . ." Legge, *A Record of Buddhistic Kingdoms*, p. 19.

p. 58: "[would] lead him . . . to enlightenment. . . ." John S. Strong, *The Experience of Buddhism* (Belmont, CA: Wadsworth Publishing, 1994), p. 324.

p. 59: "Your daughter has offered her arms. . . ." Strong, *The Experience of Buddhism*, p. 325.

p. 61: "If a man given up to capital punishment. . . ." H. Kern, trans. *Saddharamapunkarika or the Lotus of the True Law* (Oxford, England: Clarendon Press, 1884), pp. 407–408. Translation slightly modified.

p. 70: "Now this Buddha [Amida] made a great vow. . . ." Edward Kamens, *The Three Jewels: A Study and Translation of Minamoto Tamnori's Sanboe* (Ann Arbor: University of Michigan Press, 1988), p. 342.

p. 72: "Where should a swordsman fix his mind. . . ." William Theodore de Bary, ed., *The Buddhist Tradition in India, China, and Japan* (New York: Vintage Books, 1972), pp. 377 and 379.

p. 74: "Formerly to amuse myself. . . ." Stephen Adiss, *The Art of Zen: Paintings and Calligraphy by Japanese Monks, 1600–1925* (New York: Harry N. Abrams, 1989), p. 99.

CHAPTER FOUR:

p. 93: "Although to bring about inner change. . . ." Quoted by José Ignacio Cabezón, "Buddhist Principles in the Tibetan Liberation Movement" in Christopher Queen and Sallie King, eds. *Engaged Buddhism* (Albany, NY: State University of New York Press), p. 309.

INDEX

Page numbers in **boldface** are illustrations.

ABOUT THE AUTHOR

SERINITY YOUNG is a research associate in the Department of Anthropology at the American Museum of Natural History in New York City. She received her PhD in comparative religion from Columbia University in 1990 and has taught at Southern Methodist University, the University of Pennsylvania, and Hunter College. She has been a Fulbright Scholar, has been a fellow at the Center for Writers and Scholars at the New York Public Library, and has done fieldwork in India, Tibet, Nepal, Sri Lanka, Pakistan, Bangladesh, and Russia. She edited *The Encyclopedia of Women and World Religion* and *An Anthology of Sacred Texts by and about Women* and is the author of *Dreaming in the Lotus: Buddhist Dream Narrative, Imagery and Practice* and *Courtesans and Tantric Consorts: Sexualities in Buddhist Narrative, Iconography, and Ritual.*